He's Leaving Home

He's Leaving Home

MY YOUNG SON BECOMES A ZEN MONK

Kiyohiro Miura
translated by Jeff Shore

Charles E. Tuttle Company
Rutland, Vermont & Tokyo, Japan

Originally published as *Chonan no Shukke*.
Copyright © 1988 by Kiyohiro Miura
Japanese original edition published in 1988 by
Fukutake Publishing Co., Ltd. English translation rights
arranged with Kiyohiro Miura through the Japan Foreign-
Rights Centre.

This translation has been selected by the Association for 100
Japanese Books.

Illustrations by J.C. Brown

Published by the Charles E. Tuttle Company, Inc.
of Rutland, Vermont & Tokyo, Japan
with editorial offices at
2-6, Suido 1-chome, Bunkyo-ku, Tokyo 112

© 1996 by Charles E. Tuttle Publishing Co., Inc.

LCC Card No. 95-61406
ISBN 0-8048-2060-0

First edition, 1996

Printed in Japan

He's Leaving Home

Part One

I was surprised when my son first told me he wanted to become a monk. It was a Sunday morning in early spring, and we were on our way to do *zazen** as usual. The new school year was about to begin, and he was just entering third grade. He looked up at me as we walked, and said, "Dad, please ask the priest about it."

It was the first time he'd ever asked for something in such a way. Usually, he didn't even speak unless spoken to. It wasn't as if the idea had just popped into his head, either. I got the feeling he'd been mulling it over for some time, and now, out it came.

Still, I didn't take his request so seriously. First, it was all so sudden. Even though I brought him with me to the zazen meetings, I never tried to get him to sit in meditation. I just took him with me as if we were spending the day together at an amusement park. Second, he was always watching "Ikkyu-san" on TV, a cartoon series about a Japanese Zen Buddhist monk. So I soon forgot my son's request.

* Meditation in the lotus position practiced by followers of Zen Buddhism.

But he didn't. "Dad, did you ask the priest about it yet?"

This was on a Sunday morning two or three weeks later, again on the way to the temple. I realized I had seen that pleading, anxious look before. Each Sunday, after zazen, we would sit together for lunch, and I would chat with the priest. At such times, my son's silent face seemed to be urging me, "C'mon, Dad. Why don't you ask now?"

And so that day at lunch I said, with a chuckle, "It seems my son wants to become a monk!" With that I felt I'd fulfilled my promise to him.

"Is that so?" came the reply, as the priest turned toward my son and broke into that unrestrained Zen smile. "Will you be a good monk?"

"Yes," replied my son as he nodded earnestly.

I was a bit flustered; I hadn't expected it to turn out like this. I thought the priest too would take it as a childish thing, no more than a joke perhaps. But for the priest it was no joke. I'd forgotten how seriously this priest takes everything, even children's concerns. I quickly added: "He's still in elementary school; who knows how he'll change? It's probably due to that cartoon series. Let's think about it again after he finishes elementary school."

"Is this because you've been watching those 'Ikkyu-san' cartoons?" the priest asked, looking kindly into my son's eyes. But my son shook his small head no.

"I see, I see. Well, you're still young. Maybe when you're a bit older." The priest then mentioned that there were affairs of the temple to consider, too, but the manner of speaking was not at all like an adult dealing with a child.

After that, when we talked about my son, the priest would look into my son's eyes and tease, saying things like, "So, Ryota, you're gonna be a monk?" and, "Hey, little bonze! Are you studying hard?"

Then I started saying, "After he begins junior high."

But I worried about how seriously the priest was taking all this.

One day as we returned from the temple I said, "If you become a Zen monk you've got to do all kinds of cleaning, wiping, and sweeping—it's a lot of work. You still want to be a monk?"

But my son, who prefers physical exercise and handicrafts over study, only nodded with a serious face and said, "Uh-huh."

As he went on to fourth, fifth, and sixth grades I continued asking him about it. But his answer never wavered. Always the same "Uh-huh." Nothing more.

During his third year of elementary school, after he had begun saying he wanted to be a monk, he said that he would start sitting zazen with the adults. We usually sat three periods of forty minutes each, but my son began stirring restlessly after a few minutes and then went outside. Soon he began to sit longer, though: first one period, then more, and by sixth grade he was sitting as long as the adults. He mastered the full-lotus posture, and could fold his legs without even using his hands. Perhaps experienced monks can do this, but people like me who began in middle age cannot get their legs up without using their hands, and even when we do we often have to readjust our posture.

I suppose his body is supple because he is still young. But aside from how he could fold his legs, it was most strange how this son of mine, who always seemed fidgety and was even the leader of the troublemakers at school, became a completely different person at the temple.

"It's because of the father," people would say. An aunt who had often taken care of him since he was born told me in a reproachful tone, "He's like this because you take him to that temple!"

What she said was true enough, but it was also true that he gladly accompanied me. That, too, was strange. Not once did he say he wouldn't go because he wanted to play with his friends. When Sunday came, he'd get the bag with his big lunch box in it, just like on a school day, and, while mother and younger sister were still sleeping, leave the house with me. I thought perhaps it was because he enjoyed stopping on the way to eat at McDonald's or at a noodle shop in the train station where we'd slurp down piping hot buckwheat noodles. And yet, once we got to the temple, it seemed a long, monotonous routine for a child.

What did he do from the time we arrived until around two o'clock, when zazen ended and we were ready for lunch? At first he drew pictures on drawing paper with crayons. Once, he was even scolded for drawing on the sliding doors. Sometimes the elderly woman who helped around the temple would take him shopping or to catch cicadas. But he was alone most of the time. Did he simply play around the priest's living quarters, surrounded by graves, weeds, and a thicket, without even feeling lonely?

He also took some coins from the offertory box, and hid a few small Buddhist statues somewhere, but I suppose this, too, was out of sheer boredom. No matter how lonely he may have been, I certainly was little help as a father. Father simply took him there and back as if it were duty. And each Sunday the son came along without a second thought.

My wife and I stumbled upon Zenkaiji Temple one day during a walk. After about ten years living as a vagabond in the United States, I returned to Japan when I was in my early thirties, married, and began living in a brand-new apartment complex built on land being developed in the Tokyo suburbs. After moving in, we'd often take walks and check out the neighborhood.

Once, while wandering around a hillside where the land had been leveled for construction, we found ourselves on the grounds of a temple. Half-hidden among the yellow day lilies abloom on the slopes were several stone Jizo* statues. The arms and faces were gone on these youthful guardian deities, which were now buried in the weeds. We learned afterwards that they'd been dumped there during the anti-Buddhist upheaval of the Meiji era.[†]

At the bottom of the slope was a large cherry tree. Below it stood a small thatched hut, and beyond that was the main hall of the temple, a bit larger but also with a thatched roof.

The temple looked as though it had been forgotten once it was built about seven hundred years ago, back in the Kamakura era.[‡] But, thanks to the recent

* A Buddhist deity charged with protecting children.
[†] 1868–1912.
[‡] 1185–1333.

land development, it seems to have been discovered anew. Surrounded now by expansive land being developed for housing lots, at the time it seemed in danger of disappearing altogether. A strange sight indeed.

"My goodness! An old temple!" I blurted out in English, since at such times of surprise and wonder it came more readily out of me than did Japanese.

My wife pointed out a slender, wizened board nailed to a pillar of the main hall and said, "It's a Zen temple."

"Look at it!" I said, still speaking English in my astonishment. The Chinese characters on the board were weathered and uneven, almost the same color as the board itself: "Zenkaiji Meditation Hall" it read.

"Unbelievable!" I proclaimed, trying to peer through the slit where the door did not fit smoothly. The darkness seemed the kind of place in which a fox might hole up.

Returning on another day to the living quarters of the temple, which we thought was vacant, one of the shoji screen doors with torn paper suddenly slid open, and there appeared not a fox, but a figure in a worn kimono. As my wife put it, "A Jizo god appeared"— an apt expression because of the boyish face, round forehead, and long, narrow eyes. Even the swarthy complexion of the temple's inhabitant resembled that of the guardian deity.

"What do you think you're doing?" the figure in an old haori coat cried out to us. Being shouted as we were on this first encounter turned out to be rather typical, for we soon learned that this Jizo was famous for yelling.

She (this Jizo was actually a nun) thought maybe we'd come to pilfer the plants or something. The priest (I should call her a Buddhist nun but she was so spirited and mannish that no one ever did; I shall call her "the priest") loved plants, and she had gathered many kinds and planted them around the temple grounds. Since anyone can enter the temple precincts from almost any direction, even if they didn't steal things, they'd often trample the plants. Hoodlums on motorbikes trespass here too, the priest told us after inviting us to the sunny side of the porch, where she made tea and smoked her pipe while we chatted.

When she had slid open the shoji screen door just a moment before, she stared at us with piercing eyes. But now, laughing as she talked, her face was transformed into a friendly, smiling Jizo. I couldn't help worrying a little about this nun living in such an unsafe, lonely place.

But then I found it very hard to believe that she was a nun at all when she said, "One young guy came in here on a motorbike. I yelled at him so loud that he flipped right over. He just left the bike where it was and hightailed it outta' here! Musta' thought he'd seen a ghost or something! Hee-hee-hee," she chuckled in a rough, deep voice.

A temple of noble history was first built on these grounds in the Heian era* by Bodhisattva Gyoki. The temple precincts had once extended around the entire neighborhood, but peasants gradually made the land their fields. After World War Two, government

* 794–1185.

maps and documents were not in order, and then farmland reform began, so the temple land shrank even further. Without a priest, it was falling apart, so the people in the community asked the nun to come and take care of it. She told us that she intended to restore the temple in her lifetime.

On the rain-stained back wall hung a board which read, in Chinese characters: "Look right under your feet!"

Slowly, word-for-word she said, "Look right under your feet—that's the essence of Zen." Then, she added: "Everyone nowadays is fixated looking ahead, always ahead. But grabbing them by the nose and making them attentive to what lies at their very feet— that's what zazen-meditation is all about."

Then she tapped her pipe on the tobacco tray.

"What is Zen?"

That question had been at the back of my mind ever since my time in the United States. In a foreign country, one is often at a loss due to ignorance of his own country. Once I was asked by an American what Zen is, but I couldn't answer. No, worse than that, I tried to dupe him. That's why this question has always remained with me.

I was doing some work as an interpreter in New York City at the time. Living near Greenwich Village, on the weekends I got in the habit of frequenting jazz coffee shops, strip joints, and other such places, wandering from one to the other. Living by oneself in Manhattan can be very lonely. If loneliness were to be measured like temperature, then in Tokyo I could withstand temperatures as low as a few degrees above freezing, provided that I wore thick clothes. But, in Manhattan, it drops way below zero. Putting my hands in my pockets to feel the warmth emanating from my body, I could just barely sense life pulsing within me. This loneliness seemed to be built right into the city itself, so that no matter how many people I was with, always and everywhere I felt a chilling draft. And, after we'd part, the gray concrete walls towered mercilessly over me. I wandered as if possessed, dating women if I could. I guess I just longed for human warmth.

One night, after hitting a couple of strip joints, I was quite drunk from the highballs I'd ordered in lieu of paying entrance fees. Out on the street again, I was accosted by two young Americans.

"What is Zen?" one of them asked. Perhaps because I was staggering around with a look of detached loneliness, I fit their image of Zen. Sick of wandering the maze of noisy strip joints with their displays of fat and flesh, now I was walking the streets and feeling sick of life itself.

I should have just said, "I don't know," but the thought of playing with their minds popped into my head. This was right when the Zen boom was beginning among young people in the States, and I had a vague idea of how popular it was, especially with the fledgling artists who gathered in the Village near New York University. These two kids looked as if they'd just gotten off the bus from their farms somewhere in Iowa or Nebraska and were eager to ask the first Oriental they saw about this "Zen" they'd heard of. So I wanted to pull their legs a bit. Then again, I myself was lonely, and wanted to talk with someone.

Pretending I'd just arrived from Japan and could hardly speak English, I acted as if I were trying to find the right words in my limited vocabulary, and, with a pronounced and very poor accent, proceeded to explain Zen. Pointing at the questioner, at myself, and at various things I said, "Jis is Zen, Jis is Zen." The other youth seemed to sense that something funny was going on. The one who'd asked was still craning his neck and staring at me.

The questioner's friend said, "Hey, he's makin' fun a' you!" and gave him a push. He looked me over for a moment, then said, "You makin' fun a' me?"

"No," I said, "Jis is Zen."

"Alright. Then I'll show you what Zen is." Saying this, he took a boxing stance.

"Cut it out," his friend said, pulling his arm back.

I said again, "Jis is Zen."

Making as if to punch me in the nose, he took a couple of jabs, but didn't make contact. Then, putting his hands down he said, "So long, 'Jis is Zen.'" As they turned and walked away, the other said, "Thanks for the good time, bud!"

Relieved, I started walking too. I stopped for another highball on the way home, but I felt miserable. I wanted to catch up with them and apologize. Maybe get their addresses, and then later tell them in a letter what Zen really is. Since then, I've come to feel that I owe them something.

I finally decided to go and do zazen the winter my son was born. Later, I came to feel this was more than just a simple twist of fate. It snowed a lot that winter, both on the day I began Zen practice and the day my son was born. It really came down the day he was born. Watching the snowflakes falling, I felt somehow that my son came down with them. His face, beaming with the silence of heaven deep within his closed eyes, seemed like Jizo's.

Watching him still in the cradle with eyes unfocused, sometimes I'd see him smile for no apparent reason. I wondered if perhaps he remembered someone's loving gaze coming through the snowy sky on that first day.

The priest, Reverend Gukai, gave me the Zen *koan** of "Mu" to work on. A monk once asked his master whether or not a dog has the Buddha nature. Even though it is written in the Buddhist sutras that all beings possess this sublime Buddha nature, the Chinese Buddhist master of the Tang dynasty named Joshu replied in the negative: that is, he simply said, "*Mu*."

"From now on, you'll meditate on the 'Mu' koan," said the priest, who was clad in Zen robes and a surplice, and sitting on the floor with a *kyosaku*† in her lap and a dignity quite unlike when we first met.

"Whether you're walking in the street, riding a train, or gazing at your child's face, be Mu. Just Mu. The seer, the seeing, and the seen are all Mu. Be alert!" Saying this, she struck my shoulders with the kyosaku.

---

* An unanswerable conundrum ("What is the sound of one hand clapping," etc.) used by Zen practitioners in their quest to achieve enlightenment.
† A warning stick with which Zen masters sometimes strike their disciples.

On a different occasion, she told me: "Zen is not just meditating on Mu, you know. It's not a trivial thing like that. Mu is just a means. If you get attached to Mu, that's dead Zen. Walking down the street is Zen, riding the train is Zen, playing with a child is Zen. The whole universe is nothing but Zen, nothing but the koan. This is called the *genjo-koan*, the koan manifest here and now."

My wife was not too happy about my going to do zazen. You see, I'd begun going without even inviting her. Once when the subject came up, she said, "You just go off by yourself, and do whatever you want. Not once did you ask me if I might want to come along."

I was shocked when I first heard this. She had spent five years in the States, and it just never occurred to me that this woman who loved hotels and restaurants would want to do zazen. Another time, she told me: "Look at the kind of person you are. Eight years in America, and what were you doing? Always taking girls out, or going to those clubs and bars. If someone like you takes up zazen, is it so strange for me to?"

"It's not like playing tennis on Sunday, or taking dancing lessons. And it's not for women, anyway. It's basically a men's thing."

"What! Isn't the priest a woman?"

That was a hard one to explain. The priest, well, she was not exactly your average woman. She hadn't a feminine bone in her body. But then again, she wasn't like your average man either, the kind that takes his wife and kids for a drive on Sundays. She was accomplished in judo and Japanese fencing, and had a scar on her forehead from a run-in with a gangster.

She even stood out in the meditation hall where she trained in the Hokuriku* area, nicknamed "The Devil's Dojo," and was so unconventional that her master had her expelled from the order. She considered it a blessing, however, and took the opportunity to make a pilgrimage around the country, visiting renowned masters. Used to living this way, she has no problem staying in this run-down old temple. Perhaps she traveled at night, listening to the high-pitched laugh of the long-nosed *tengu*.† (She said they cross the valleys in groups.) She must have done ascetic practices, like meditating under a waterfall, for some time, and continued her zazen under trees and on rocks.

Maybe during this time her sexual nature underwent a transformation. I can't help but think so. Seeing this priest, I understand well that sexual distinctions are essentially relative.

"I'm not a woman!" she'd say. Then she would tell the story of how much trouble she caused at the "men's only" monk's training hall when she would walk right into the men's bathhouse.

"Women are no good," she often said. "I came to understand that women are not cut out for such training. In the beginning, I thought it important for women to find salvation, so I trained hard for some

---

* A region in central Honshu including Fukui, Ishikawa, Niigata, and Toyama prefectures.
† Goblins from Japanese folklore.

time. But we always quit halfway. Even though we may have a clear goal at first, it fades away after a while. That's the way women are. Women have strong desires. Zazen is throwing everything away. Women, though, can't help but pick things up, like when they see vegetables dropped on the ground. A woman's strongest desire is toward her children. When it comes to their own children, they're utterly blind—they can't tell shit from soup.

"Mr. Kimura," she turned toward me, "you're a man but you take good care of your child." She added with a disinterested look, "you're rather unique."

I took my son to the temple not because I took good care of him, as the priest suggested; rather, it was the result of my not taking care of him. At least that's what my wife thinks. Other husbands stay home on Sundays and play catch with their children or take them fishing. I used to leave my elementary school son and preschool daughter and be out of the house before anybody was even up. Worse still, the night before, I would make my wife prepare enough sandwiches to feed five people! (I never asked her to make me sandwiches instead of the usual box lunch, but she kept on making them. She had to make enough for five people, because we all shared our lunches.)

Soon there was rebellion in the ranks. But it wasn't from my wife. It was from my son. He'd sneak into neighbors' houses and munch away on their sweets, or shoplift with his buddies. My son was the kind of kid that would jump right off a cliff if someone told him to.

"He's such a restless boy. Why, he's as much trouble as three kids his age. I just can't handle him by myself. And I have to take care of Rie too." When my wife told me of his wild behavior I was quite upset.

At the next zazen gathering, I stated that I was going to absent myself for a while to take care of my son. The priest's response was immediate. "Bring him with you. He can be as wild as he wants at this temple. Children get wild because they're always being told, 'Don't do this, don't do that.' You even restrict what he eats, don't you. Always making him eat that health food like you were feeding a rabbit. You don't feed that growing boy the food he likes, so he goes to the neighbor's looking for some. If he came here, I'd let him eat whatever he wanted. We have so many sweets here, they're always going bad on us. If kids can eat as much as they want, they'll stop desiring it."

All I could do was bow my head and mutter, "Thank you."

When I asked my son if he wanted to go to the temple, he was delighted. Maybe he had wondered what kind of interesting place I was off to every Sunday. I figured he would tire of it before long, but instead he started coming to wake me on Sunday mornings

Soon enough, though, a problem occurred. One of the zazen old-timers complained, "This isn't a nursery school. He's disturbing our zazen."

The priest summoned the lay representative of the zazen gatherings, the head of a wholesale seafood outlet. She demanded, "Just who's the master and who's the disciple around here? I said it was OK. I have something in mind for him. What kind of zazen is that anyway, if it gets disturbed by one child?" I heard this from the woman who helps take care of the priest.

I have something in mind for him. What did the priest mean by that? I wondered about it, but not enough to ask her. If she had already foreseen that he would become a monk, I must say she had quite an eye. But she might have meant something else, because she never once told me to make him sit zazen. Sometimes she amazed us with her well-honed intuition, which seemed to be a result of her Zen training.

Sometimes, at the end of *dokusan*,* she would say things like, "Recently you've been off your guard. That's why you haven't been making any progress," and, "Don't let your mind wander when you're sitting." Then she would strike the tatami mat with her kyosaku.

And she was right. When I was supposed to be just sitting, I was in fact daydreaming about buying new audio equipment or thinking about places to take my family driving during my time off. To make up for this, during dokusan I would bow extra carefully or shout enthusiastically. But it never worked.

When my son first said he wanted to be a monk I thought about how all this had come to pass, and wondered at the strangeness of it. I just happened to discover the temple during a walk, then began going to do zazen. Then my son, whom I'd abandoned at home, started coming with me and eventually came to want to live there. It all sounds natural enough.

* A private audience granted by a Zen master to a disciple.

But that it came together in this way—I can think of no other word to express it than "fate."

One other thing I must add about this priest Gukai— known in town as "the crazy monk"—is that she's an animal lover. I don't mean as spoiled pets either. It's the animals that are attracted to her, and so she feels affection for them. That's the type of animal lover she is. Put simply, she understands them.

All kinds of animals would meander in and settle down for a while at the priest's side, then wander off: chickens, small birds, rabbits, quails, ducks, goats, not to mention dogs and cats. Most of them were brought in by the parishioners, or the farmers in the neighborhood. They'd say they didn't want them anymore, or ask the priest to take care of them for a while.

She never pampered them or spoiled them like pet lovers do, treating them as if they were human. Animals were simply animals to her. They were free to stay or to go. All she did was talk to them.

And they seemed to have no trouble understanding her. Some years ago, a canary showed up, and they used to talk up a storm. When a certain cat would approach, the canary would speed up its chatter as if to inform on the intruder or try to drive it out. Eventually, the canary disappeared, and the priest gave the cat a good scolding, thinking it had gotten its revenge on the canary. It seems the cat felt really dejected, and soon it disappeared as well. The priest told us it had probably wandered off the temple grounds and been attacked by a stray dog.

Then, one day, as the priest was walking on the road outside the temple, she heard a cat's meow. She looked around, but no sign of it. If she started walking again, it would start meowing again. Then she realized it was the cry of the cat that had disappeared. Searching in the bushes nearby, she found the rotted carcass of a cat. She dug a hole in the ground, buried the corpse, and recited the Heart Sutra.

She had that kind of side to her. I felt that my son's not getting bored while playing at the temple, and also his coming to want to live there, had something to do with the kind of person she was.

My biggest worry was whether or not he was fit to be a monk. I think of a monk as someone with deep compassion for others, not concerned with physical comforts or possessions, willing to get down on his knees and scrub the floors. Then, if he has time, he would try and read the entire collection of Buddhist sutras. As for my son's compassion, well, maybe it'll come with adulthood. I can't say he's unconcerned with material possessions, either; he wants all the things his friends have: a bicycle, roller skates, a Walkman, and so on. Recently, he's been eyeing those fancy motorcycles. When I'm driving, he sits in the passenger seat and imitates me. "Sure wish I could take driving lessons,"he'll say.

I don't worry too much about all the cleaning and sweeping that a Zen monk has to do, because my son is so restless to begin with. He is more likely to get moving if I tell him to clean something than if I tell him to crack a book and study. I'm afraid the vast collection of Buddhist sutras will remain beyond his reach. Might as well forget about his becoming the kind of scholar-monk who goes to India to study ancient scriptures, or gives lectures on Zen classics.

Watching him sitting in the passenger seat pretending to drive while he listens to his Walkman, I wondered what on earth made him want to be a monk. I just stared at him in spite of myself. Did he think he'd be able to drive around in a car listening to his Walkman as a monk? That priest will never let him do such a thing, so I feel bad for him.

"It's only natural that a child wants things," the priest said. "But it's the parents that made him that way in the first place. A growing child tries to take everything into himself. And it's the duty of the parents to teach him to distinguish what's necessary from what's not."

A friend told me: "Haven't the priests themselves always been greedy? Making the journey to India for the sake of sacred texts at the risk of great personal sacrifice—why that's one out of ten thousand priests, and one in a hundred years. You're too idealistic. Besides, it's good to have desires. Because one desires, one can attain enlightenment. If he had no desires to begin with, he wouldn't make much of a priest."

"Ryota wants everything you want," my wife said.

I said, "I've thought a lot about what Ryota should be when he grows up. At first, I thought an actor or a jazz drummer. He likes to express himself with his body, move with the rhythm. He really came alive playing drums at the school festival, although it was just an extracurricular activity. Then again, I thought about him working for a bank or a trading company, being a store owner or in public service, but they never seemed quite right for him. I had a friend, a really successful businessman with beautiful shops in Tokyo and New York and a wife who was a runner-up in the Miss Japan beauty contest. Well, in the midst of that jet-set life, one day he up and killed himself."

"You're always so negative. Working for a trading company or a bank is not such a trivial thing. All the wives in our housing development are proud of their husbands. It's not right for you to turn everything into a statistic with your twisted logic."

"I've thought it through from the historical point of view, as well. How many millions and billions of humans have appeared on this planet and then disappeared. And every one of them was once a child like Ryota, thinking and worrying about what he should be while his parents also worried. Very few can lead the life they wish, while the vast majority have no choice. And of those few, how very few, have left their mark in history. But are they the only ones who really count? If Ryota makes a bit of a mistake in this choice, it's only a problem for him and for us, his parents."

Even though I saw the annoyed look on my wife's face, I kept on talking. "Anyway, who can decide which path is really the right one to take? The path's not made until he walks it. And he's the only one who can walk it.

"From my historical sense, I feel certain that Japan's current prosperity is about to run into a dead end. Look at America; Japan will eventually be like that. While drugs and sex crimes are on the rise, in the mountains of California there are Zen centers forming and many youngsters go there. Not just youngsters either. Did you know that the former governor of California quit being governor and went to a temple in Kyoto to do zazen?"

"So, since Americans are doing zazen, our son's got to become a Zen monk, is that it?" my wife interjected.

"No, what I'm saying is that we're entering a religious age. Science, economics, politics cannot go on ignoring religion. That physicist in America, Fritzof Capra, says that what physicists are now thinking is the same as Oriental religion. When I told the priest that, she said she knew it all along."

My wife responded, "I don't know about Zen, physics, and all that complicated stuff. It doesn't matter to me one way or the other. I don't care if he becomes a businessman or a monk. As long as our son can live as he likes and doesn't trouble others I'm happy. A son eventually has to leave home anyway and stand on his own two feet. If he comes by once a week to see us, that's fine. He could do that living in the temple, couldn't he? Maybe he could return for the new year. And summer vacation, too. I'll leave his room just as it is, his desk and chair just like they are, so whenever he returns he can use them. It would be a pity if his things were to get lost, or if he had no place of his own."

I imagined him home for a brief summer vacation or at the new year, walking in the hallway of our apartment, wearing monk's robes and with head shaved. It reminds me of *yabu-iri*, a word I often heard in my youth. It means "some time off for shop apprentices to return home." I don't know if the word is used for apprentice monks though. If one of the housewives in the apartment complex runs into him, she's sure to stare in amazement. Then the rumors will start: Why is it that the son has gone off and become a monk when the father is not a temple priest? The parents even make him walk around town in those old-fashioned, black work pants. Not long ago, he looked just fine wearing a bright sports shirt, white pants, and blue sneakers. Maybe they had some bad karma, so the parents made him become a monk.

He'll stand at the entrance to our apartment and, bowing like a guest, he'll say in a loud voice, just as the priest taught him, "Mother and father, please pardon the temporary inconvenience."

And if we inquire about his health or the temple, I know all we'll get are textbook answers like "Yes," and, "That's correct."

I also pictured our family of four—Mom, Dad, son, and little daughter Rie—sitting in front of our Buddhist altar at home, with him taking the lead in reading sutras. (Actually, our "Buddhist altar" consisted of a small Jizo statue—a gift from the priest—on top of a shelf, an old teabowl which served as an incense holder, and an ordinary vase with a spray of flowers. The posthumous Buddhist names of our ancestors were written on strips of paper which we had pasted on the wall.) The image of us gathered together like that was somewhat gloomy, and yet there was something alluring about it too.

And what about the strict discipline and lifestyle? I once saw a TV program about life at Eiheiji Monastery: Before dawn, a young monk runs through the long, dark hallways, ringing a handbell to awaken everyone. Zazen in the freezing dawn, with steam rising from bald heads. Barefoot, wiping the floors

with a damp rag. It looked incredibly severe, a world completely isolated from this one. But the priest said that it's not like that once you're inside. Things that are difficult to do can be accomplished easily in a large group. Isn't that the kind of world for my son to live in, since he makes friends quickly and is easily influenced by them?

Once one enters that world, it would be of no use at all to try and measure it with the yardstick of this one. Perhaps he'll even stop wanting to own things like stereos and motorcycles.

On the TV program, one of the monks at Eiheiji was asked: "What do you enjoy here?" The interviewer asked this with a tone of suspicion as to why one would leave a world full of pleasures to hole up and struggle in a place like this. I still remember the response of the young monk, who at the time was assigned the task of working in the kitchen from morning to night, preparing the meals for the other monks. Tilting his shaven head a bit, he said: "Maybe the joy of preparing something well today that I couldn't prepare well yesterday."

Then, seeming to ignore this response, the program shot to another scene.

But that answer impressed me deeply. Man can find joy under any conditions. And it's those small joys that keep us going. Perhaps, more than "joys," we should call them "appreciations"—thankfulness. Compared with these, how unstable and fleeting are the joys of sexual love, or winning a lottery. The greater the joy, the more short-lived it is. Anyway, all joys are ephemeral, so we shouldn't hold onto them too tightly. One day my son will understand that.

The joy of preparing something well today that I couldn't prepare well yesterday.

When my son understands that, maybe he'll become a real monk. As I was contemplating such things, my son's idea of actually becoming a monk gradually started to take root.

Once he entered junior high school, though, he started acting strange. Telltale cigarette butts turned up in his pencil case and girlie magazines were found in his schoolbag. He began going to school leaving the stand-up collar of his jacket unbuttoned, and the end of his belt hanging down at his side instead of in the belt loops. He wore sneakers as if they were sandals—with the back part stepped on—and carried a brightly colored shopping bag rather than his schoolbag.

I thought it was just a temporary adjustment problem with his new school and all, but then his homeroom teacher paid a visit and told us to beware because our son was hanging around with the known troublemakers at school. Just as I was beginning to grasp the gravity of the situation, a fight broke out with students from another school. My wife was called in and informed who the leader of the gang was: our son.

Through all this, he continued going with me to the temple every Sunday for zazen, carrying his big lunch box in a bag, and following me with his usual uninterested look as if nothing had changed. He rarely talked to me the whole time we were cleaning the temple garden, doing zazen, eating a late lunch, or returning home. But it is a rule for Zen practice that, during these times, even parent and child should not engage in unnecessary talk, so I wasn't too concerned.

The only change was that he wanted to go back early, to get together with his friends. Once in a while, he finished up lunch quickly and then took the train back by himself. Since elementary school he had never gone on Sundays to play ball, or go fishing or on excursions with his friends even when they asked him. Once he started junior high, I thought he should, though, so I sent him off from the temple with a smile and a "Have a good time." But then he would get in fights.

"How could you get in a fight after doing zazen?" I scolded him. It was pathetic. I guess after zazen he did things like smoke and leaf through girlie magazines with his friends.

His grades were slipping, and he was now second or third from the bottom of his class. His homeroom teacher told us that he'd make wisecracks during class to get the other students to laugh. "Why don't you keep quiet in class? If they laugh, it's only because they think you're stupid!" I chided him.

He could sit without saying a word for two hours in zazen on Sundays, why not in school? "I just can't," he'd say.

One day, I warned him about not studying. "Being a monk doesn't mean just cleaning and sweeping, you know. You've got to be able to study some, too."

Then he finally began saying it: "I'm not gonna be a monk."

"Then what are you going to be?" I demanded.

He seemed stuck for words. "I'll find something that's right for me."

I shouted, "Stupid! You've got a lot of nerve saying 'something that's right' for you when you don't even study."

I tossed and turned in bed that night, sick with worry over the thought that now he won't even become a monk. I hadn't realized how much I'd pinned my hopes for him on it, how much I'd anticipated it. Realizing that he might not become one at all made me think what a wonderful thing it is to be a monk. It's something so very few can aspire to, something so very few have a chance to do. An ordinary boy like my son could shoot for nothing higher. It seemed something had been taking him by the hand and leading him in that direction. Maybe he was destined since birth, maybe now the Jizo in our family altar was leading him. Was this Jizo losing its effect, or were the bad influences now surrounding him too powerful? I must somehow get him out of that ring of evil influences, I thought. That's the first priority, whether he becomes a monk or not. If he came to hate the thought of being a monk and instead went the route of Everyman, that's the way it had to be. But if he simply continued the way he was, he'd be defeated by those bad influences.

I spoke with my wife about transferring him to another school. We considered sending him to a private school that had stricter rules than the public school he goes to now. He'd have to take a special entrance exam for transfer students, but the real problem was his grades. What kind of private school would admit him when he was second or third from the bottom of his class? And if he got in someplace, it'd probably be some third- or fourth-rate school that didn't have enough applicants. Then he might get even worse. There was hope, however: a denominational school. He might have a chance at a school affiliated with a religious denomination.

My wife and I went to see the priest. "Oh, my goodness. The two of you! Something big must be cooking," she said with a hint of sarcasm, as we bowed to her.

I told her what had been happening, and that our son was now saying he didn't want to be a monk.

"Well, he's been living in such a pure world up until recently. Now all kinds of germs are starting to stick to him, but I wouldn't be too concerned about it. He'll change again soon enough," the priest said casually, as a smile played across her boyish face.

I mentioned our idea of transferring him to another school. The priest responded, "Sounds good. You should try to keep him away from bad influences as much as possible."

Then I mentioned the Sendan School, and she said, "That's a Buddhist school, although many children from lay families also go. Children of temple families used to get admitted without even taking the exam, but I've heard that's changed now."

I said I thought it was fine if he became a monk. That was what he'd wanted to do after entering junior high, anyway. But while his parents were hesitating, he'd changed his mind. I added that if he transferred to this school and regained his interest in being a monk, that would be just fine.

"I see," she said, looking at me with eyes bright. She turned toward my wife. "And you agree with this?"

"Yes," my wife said, bowing her head.

"Then it's decided!" the priest called out in the loudest voice I'd ever heard her use. "Now, leave it up to me."

That was quick, I thought. Her handling of the situation was quite unexpected; I was used to seeing her sit and drink tea while she chatted with guests for hours at a time, as if she'd sunk roots clear through the tatami mat.

I heard that the following Sunday, when my son entered the dokusan room for his private interview, the priest asked, "Are you still interested in being a monk?"

My son said, "Yes, I am . . . but . . . " he hesitated.

"What's the matter?" she asked.

"I don't have any confidence."

"Why?"

"Because my father says that somebody like me could never be a monk." (My heart really ached when I heard that, for I understood my son's confusion only too well.)

Then the priest told him, "Well, I'm going to make you into one good monk."

Then, at lunchtime, she said, "I have an important announcement to make," and proceeded to tell the members of the zazen gathering about Ryota's becoming a monk. The priest emphasized, "It was his own decision."

"Oh!" everyone cried out in admiration.

"And he must take responsibility for it," she said,

aiming this last remark toward my son as he squirmed on the edge of his seat, then nodded meekly.

The priest phoned the Sendan School, set up an appointment with the principal, then marched in with me. Students in uniform were coming out of the front gate, and down the avenue lined with ginkgo trees. When they saw the priest in her Buddhist robes, they removed their hats and bowed to her. My son's school was not like this at all, and I was pleasantly surprised at the difference.

The principal appeared in the reception room wearing a suit with a surplice over it. He joined his hands together, and bowed his shaved head to the priest. The priest then introduced me. "This is the father of Kimura Ryota, the boy who decided to take the examination for transfer students." Then, she stated, "It has been decided that he will become a monk and eventually succeed me as resident priest of Zenkaiji Temple. That is why we have come here today."

It seemed to interest the principal that a boy from a lay family would want to be a monk. He asked the priest, "Is he a relative?"

"No. We're not doing this to keep the temple in the family. It is the boy's own desire. He's been coming to my temple ever since he was a first-grader, and when he was in third grade he first said he wanted to become a monk. We told him he's too young, wait until junior high. In the meantime, we waited to see whether he would change his mind, but he never did. Finally we gave in," she said, that unrestrained Zen smile of hers breaking across her face.

"Well, well," said the principal, who seemed quite impressed. "And does he do zazen?"

"Same as the adults. And his devotions are most sincere. Nothing like an adult's. He's so pure, he does them with all his heart. It's quite extraordinary."

"Really? Nowadays it's hard to find someone who can do devotions like that, even among the monks," he sighed. Then, he changed the subject. "By the way, has he already had his ordination ceremony? If he enters our school he'll also be joining our religious association, and he must be ordained to do that," he said, looking at the priest and then at me. "You might laugh, but recently more and more parishioners have sought introductions to our school through their temples, to get their children away from the delinquency problems in the public junior high schools. I tell you this in strictest confidence though . . . "

"He'll be ordained soon," the priest replied calmly.

"Hmm." She turned towards me, and smiled, "I had thought of doing it a little later, but maybe sooner is better." She had never mentioned it to me, so all I could do was mutter a vague "Uh-huh."

"Well then, how about after the temple services for the spring equinox?"

"There's really no need to hurry," the principal offered. Then he added, "As long as it's decided that he will be ordained, anytime before the summer vacation would be fine. During summer vacation, students will be training together, so as long as he's been tonsured by then . . . "

"Well, it's got to be done anyway, so let's do it soon. How about it, Mr. Kimura?"

"Yes, that's fine" was all I could say, since I knew nothing about such monkish matters.

The principal then walked us through the corridors to the entrance. Unlike in public schools, the wooden floors here were so polished I feared I might slip and fall. The principal praised the virtues of a boy like Ryota who comes from a lay family, yet applies to this school and becomes a monk.

I was getting anxious, and I voiced my anxiety over whether my son would fit in with all the children from temple families, but the principal said that his concern was just the opposite. I asked him what he meant, and with a really worried expression, he replied that there were some bad kids from temple families whom he felt might frustrate my son's noble intentions. I wanted to say he needn't worry, but held back.

"Well, I think everything's OK," the priest said to me as I drove back.

I replied, "There's still the entrance exam," afraid that the results might spoil the principal's image of Ryota.

The priest didn't seem concerned about that at all. She seemed completely preoccupied with the sudden prospect of a successor. Removing her sandals, she sat up in the passenger seat, talking nonstop as she chain-smoked cigarettes and dropped the ashes into the portable ashtray she held in her lap. She went on like this the whole way back to the temple, a ninety-minute trip. She certainly was loquacious. I occasionally chimed in, as I rolled the windows up and down to let out the smoke.

"I had thought of retiring, but now it looks like my

work is cut out for me, eh, Mr. Kimura? I guess this is all part of Buddha's grand design. I have some money put away for retirement, but that money could get him through graduate school. This may be part of Buddha's plan, too. What comes up later can be discussed later."

I told her that I intended at least to pay his school expenses.

"No, no, you mustn't do that. It's a monk's duty to take care of himself. It would be corrupt for a monk to receive financial assistance from the laity. Receiving alms and offerings—that's different; they're for performing funeral services and the like. To think of paying a monk's way is conceited. Put it out of your mind right now."

"Well, if you say so," I replied.

"Mr. Kimura, I want that boy to be a monk like Dogen Zenji, the founding leader of our Soto branch of Zen Buddhism. You might laugh, but I want him to approach as much as he can the greatness of Dogen. This is the vow of every Soto Zen monk. I think there are two kinds of monks: the one that seeks high rank in the priesthood, and the one that becomes a worthy monk. The high-ranking priests move up the administrative ladder of sect affairs; the worthy monks concentrate on religious practice and attain profound Awakening. Which one do you prefer?"

"The worthy monk, of course."

"You bet. But those worthy monks are poor!" she laughed. "I intend to really train him. Nothing half-assed. In the world today all you see are half-assed people. Even most monks are, nowadays. Monks are easily given certificates of enlightenment. You can't trust such things. Recently, all you have to do is sit for awhile and you get your certificate of enlightenment. It's the master's fault, too. I'm going to be strict, though. Listen, Mr. Kimura, however cruel it may seem, you must keep quiet and not interfere. Can you do that?"

"Yes, I can."

"My biggest concern is whether my own strength will hold out. Him, he's still young. But just telling him what to do is not enough; if I don't go through it with him from early morning I won't be able to truly train him. I'm old, and weak from illness. Don't know when my number will be up. But then that doesn't matter. I think of this as my final work."

Then she puffed on her cigarette. "The rest of my life will be devoted to training him. He won't do me any good, but he will be of service to the temple. That's what the fortuneteller told me the other day. And that's fine with me.

"I thought about a good Buddhist name for him, and even went to a fortuneteller who specializes in creating provident names to suit people. What do you think about the name Ryokai? The Chinese character for *kai* is from my name, Gukai, and the one for *ryo* is from his given name, Ryota."

"Sounds good."

"Ryokai is a fine, gentle name. Suits his personality well. By the way, it seems that the name Kimura Ryokai is not so good. He has a tendency to get wild, and naming him that is like adding oil to the flame. His high spirits are good, but he's too loose. The fortuneteller even said he's likely grow up to be a womanizer."

I couldn't help laughing. "Might be right about that!"

"Yes. That fortuneteller's good; been giving me advice for a long time now. Asked him if I should give my surname of Gyokusen to your son, and he said it was perfect—it would help to restrain his bad tendencies. He's a boy so he should have many friends, yet he mustn't be too indiscreet. What do you think: Gyokusen Ryokai?"

"Seems fine to me."

"If you don't approve just say so, and we'll leave his surname as it is. Although I must say it doesn't go well with his new given name."

I figured he was to become a temple child anyway. I don't know of any young monks who commute daily from their homes. And if he's going to spend the rest of his life in a temple, it would be best to have a Buddhist name. It will help smooth the transition to his new life. Changing his name doesn't mean he becomes another person. Anyway, whatever is best for my son.

With my hands on the wheel, I bowed my head: "Please take good care of him."

"Even though the name is changed, the parent is still the parent. The fact that you are the father will never change. A name is only a label anyway. Did you know that the surname I use now, Gyokusen, was actually given to me? I was born with the surname Ichinoseki, the only daughter of an innkeeper at a stopover point on the Hokurikudo."

Her life seems to have been a very stormy one. She's told me bits from time to time but it has so many ups and downs that I haven't been able to put it all together. It seems she was given the surname Gyokusen by people having a dispute about who would take over as head of an old family in the Chugoku* area. When she was on pilgrimage there, she helped them to settle the discord in the family, although I don't know the details. They told her she would be doing them a great favor if she took on the name, so she did. Even if my son inherits that name, then, it doesn't mean that he's been adopted into that family. It's just a label, after all.

Eight applicants took the special exam for transfer students at Sendan Junior High School, and only two passed. My son was one of them. We waited in a room at the school while the applicants were called in one by one. Anxious, I wondered, Will we be next, will we be next? Finally, there were only two applicants left, so I figured there was no hope. But it turned out that the two remaining were the successful ones. When I showed the certificate of admission to my son, he gave it a strange stare.

"You passed," I said.

"I did it!" he cried out.

Looking at his face, I realized that although he had had a blast at his former junior high, he seemed really delighted about entering a new one. And I was more delighted with his success than I was when I first saw my own acceptance announcement for university.

The other successful applicant wore thick glasses and seemed the studious type; he took the news

* A region in western Honshu including Hiroshima, Okayama, Shimane, Tottori, and Yamaguchi prefectures.

lightly. But his plump father, a postmaster, was over-joyed and handed me his calling card. Maybe he should've made some up for his son, too, so then he could have passed them around. I had the feeling that of the two students accepted today, one had gotten the highest test score, the other the lowest.

Then came the ordination ceremony.

The priest won't take second best, so when she could not acquire the desired priest's robes and things in Tokyo, she simply ordered them from Kyoto. She called an assistant monk from a temple connected with hers to help, invited the parish leader and all the members of the weekly zazen group, and did her best to hold the ceremony in the ancient, traditional style. Our son spent the night before at the temple. The assistant monk prepared a ceremonial bath for him to wash away all the worldly dirt and troubles that had accumulated on him until now. That day, something occurred which, at least for us, his parents, was a most serious event. His grandparents and we were to attend the ceremony, but my wife also wanted to invite his aunt who had taken care of him when he was young. My wife telephoned, and the aunt said she would definitely come. When I heard this, I thought we had better call the temple to get permission.

"Don't go inviting all kinds of people!" the priest snapped. "There are plenty of other people I'd like to invite. This isn't a show, you know. It's a ceremony in which the child cuts his ties with his parents. To tell you the truth I didn't even want you to invite the grandparents, but, well, I let that slide. But this is not something for all the relatives."

When my wife heard this, she said she couldn't possibly tell dear Auntie, so I called and explained that she could not attend because it was a ceremony to cut his ties.

"You mean his ties with me, too, don't you," she said in a disgusted tone.

Sure enough, the ceremony began with our son's announcing his parting from his parents. Wearing his school uniform, he entered the main hall with palms together in prayer, accompanied by the assistant monk. My wife and I were sitting together near the inner sanctuary.

He approached by himself and sat down in front of me. He then placed his palms on the tatami and spoke: "Father, you have taken care of me for a long time. Thank you."

Then, he rose and sat in front of my wife: "Mother, you have taken care of me for a long time. Thank you."

He bowed his head.

Next, he walked over to the priest, got down on his knees, and again pressed his palms together. She stated the precepts one by one, and each time asked whether he would keep them. In a loud voice, he proclaimed each time, "Yes I shall."

Then, the priest chanted sutras, while he was given a surplice, robes, and traditional undergarments, one after the other. When that was over, he left the room.

After about fifteen minutes, he reentered in white dress, and with head shaved. The transformation from hair and uniform to shaven pate and white

cloth was quite dramatic, like the "quick change" during a kabuki performance.

My wife's eyes were red now. Looking at him in the white cloth, I really felt that he'd gone to a world beyond our reach. Yet, it seemed so sudden, so unreal somehow. Have the ties between parents and child really been cut? Is that relation such an empty thing?

"Thank you father, thank you mother"—just saying that nullifies everything up until now? What is a parent-child relationship? Are the ties between parent and child no more than an illusion? Mere *idée fixe* born of convention? Are parents and children just playing roles?

Listening to the sutras being chanted I felt I had been given one big koan to wrestle with. Looking at the entranced priest as she chanted, it seemed that the lips on this Jizo face were the only things moving, like small creatures.

Those lips seemed to be saying: "Mu, Muuuuuu—"

The ordination ceremony was over, but our son still lived at home. We'd made a deal with the priest that he'd stay with us until he graduated junior high. This was best for the temple, as well, since it would be too much trouble for them to have a boy of that age to look after. So we all decided to have him stay at home in the meantime.

The ceremony is over. Now he has returned here to the home he left just yesterday, but he waits at the entrance. Before removing his shoes, he stands straight and announces, shaved head bowed slightly, "I will be under your care for awhile."

We can no longer call him Ryota. "It must be Ryo-kai." We had been warned about this by Reverend Gukai. If we inadvertently call him Ryota, he protests, "Please call me Ryokai."

He is serious about it. And he was deadly serious at the ceremony, too. For us, his parents, it hasn't quite sunk in—the reality of it hasn't hit us yet. So we end up slipping and calling him Ryota.

His "Ryokai" response to this is so interesting that I find myself occasionally calling him by his former name on purpose. But, as I gradually get used to calling him by his new name, I find a wondrous change. It is as if calling him Ryokai instead of Ryota has caused a different character to emerge from him: Ryokai never says things like "Whaddaya want?" or "Leave me alone, stupid."

He no longer kicks off his shoes, throws his school-bag around, or leaves his dirty underwear on the floor. Upon his return from school, Ryokai announces, "I'm home."

At meals he puts his palms together and says, "Thank you for this food."

Before bed, he washes the underwear he wore that day, and hangs them to dry. It seems as if calling him by that name creates an atmosphere of respect between us.

Other than that, however, his behavior hasn't changed at all. He still lies on the floor in front of the TV, chin in hand, and watches "Doraemon" cartoons, or listens to cassette tapes of Off Course and Arabesque. According to little sister Rie, he dances to disco music when his parents aren't around. When he studies, he always has his Walkman headphones on his shaved head.

When I see him like this, I wonder if maybe he took his vows too early. But then again, if he hadn't done when he did, he might have ended up worse that he is now.

The time I feel most strongly that he has indeed "left home to take religious vows" is when we are out together. That shaved head stands out anywhere. I figured he wouldn't be with us at home much longer, so occasionally we would go out for a drive or to a family restaurant—things he loved doing. But that fair-skinned boy with shaved head attracted attention everywhere. Once in a while, the hushed voices of elementary school kids would reach us: "He must be training for a sports tournament or something."

When we went to do zazen on Sundays, he wore a monk's black work clothes and his surplice. Since I wore regular clothes when I accompanied him, he seemed to attract even more stares. I felt like I had taken the easy way, while my son was made to suffer. Why did those black work clothes seem to symbolize suffering? I felt pity for him in such situations, but he was surprisingly unaffected. To think that he used to like wearing a name-brand sport shirt with white jeans. Is this also the result of his name change?

The temple children hated having their heads shaved, so they came to school with long hair. Some disliked their Buddhist names and adopted common Japanese names. Hearing that our son had left his lay home so he could enter the priesthood, one of them sneered, "What an idiot! If you want a temple so much, you can have mine."

Ryokai came home and told us this with an amused air.

Another day, I went for some event at school. The students were marching, and there, amid the sea of black heads, was a single white one resembling an egg bobbing up and down. I had a sudden urge to call out, "Ryokai!"

There certainly were some disadvantages though. For example, family matters became temple affairs. We often forgot that Ryokai was now a child of the temple, and he would start talking about just about anything. That was another habit of his that did not change.

"Been to that family restaurant again yesterday, Mr. Kimura? Your family really likes eating out, don't they," the priest said with that smile of hers.

"Bought a new car, did you? One of those fancy jobs with all those buttons. Took out another loan to do it, eh? The banks are lending more and more money, and everybody's tripping over their own feet to take out a loan so they can buy something they don't even need. The only ones benefiting are those bankers!

"What's your monthly salary? Three hundred thousand, maybe four hundred thousand yen? You got any money in your account? No? Raking in four hundred thousand yen a month, but you've got nothing stashed away. And you're having trouble paying the mortgage on your house. Then, you go and buy a new car. You're really bad at managing money. You'd never survive as a monk. It's had a bad influence on Ryokai, too.

"What do you think our monthly income is here at the temple? Two hundred thousand yen a month. You may not believe it, but it's true. Sometimes we receive a bit more; it depends on the month. And, with that, we have to manage this temple and grounds of over ten thousand square meters. Not many people, but plenty of dogs, cats, and birds. I have a gardener come in, and I have to buy flowers, incense, clothes, and things. Priests need money, too. But I don't buy any food. Here, we just eat what is given to us. Some months I think, if only we could receive three hundred thousand yen, it'd be a lot easier."

Thus, when Ryota became Ryokai, the first thing he learned was not how to read sutras or perform funeral services, but how to balance his books. He has to put down every yen that he receives and spends, then the priest checks it. Once he starts living at the temple, he'll have to do this every night, and she won't let him sleep until the accounts balance. He won't even be able to buy a soft drink on the sly at school.

I must admit though, with all this talk of frugality, I have my doubts about where all the money to equip the temple and keep it in good repair comes from. A religious corporation like the temple has certain tax advantages, I suppose, and she is strict with the money donated by the parishioners, and with the fees received for the upkeep of the graves. (The sharp contrast between the rising prosperity of the temple and her own frugal lifestyle is a puzzle nobody can figure out. Some of the parishioners say that when she was young and on pilgrimage, she used her spiritual powers to help an influential landowner in distress, and now he helps support the temple. But that is just a rumor. At any rate, during the fifteen years I've been going there to do zazen, it has undergone a transformation. No longer is it the beat-up old temple that a fox might scamper out of. Not only is there a gorgeous canopy decorating the inside of the main hall, but the priest has had imposing living quarters built on the hill where the Jizo statues once lay buried in the weeds. The place where young bikers used to trespass is now a path adorned with many new statues, showered with cherry blossoms every spring, and bathed in green every summer. The main gate of the temple, with a framed wooden sign announcing "Komyo Mountain: Zenkaiji Temple" in green ink, now stands on a path that people used to wander through at will. The dense growth of weeds has become Reverend Gukai's "botanical garden": a slew of unidentified plants and flowers collected during her peregrinations through the neighboring hills, now sprouting blossoms, fruits, and berries.)

Part Two

And now the day for Ryokai to leave home has finally arrived.

"He'll only need the clothes on his back," the priest had told us, so we just packed some things he used every day and put them in the car. My wife said that we should at least buy him new bedding. But then I remembered the priest had stated, "Monks sleep anywhere," so I gritted my teeth and replaced his with mine. The only thing the priest asked us to bring was a desk lamp for him to study by.

The Walkman that he always listened to while studying and a bunch of music tapes which he had recorded were considered necessities, so we put them in a bag to take along. As we were packing I decided to take his stereo too. Fortunately, the priest likes music: she has a collection of old albums, recordings of sermons, and the like, and she mentioned to me that she'd like to listen to them someday.

I had told her, "Ryokai likes Bach. It's religious music."

So, I added my Bach and other classical records to his rock albums and took the whole bunch. I don't know what kind of music he'll play at the temple, but perhaps she'll think it's Bach. Ryokai really loves toccata and fugue pieces, and Bach's "Jesu Joy of Man's Desiring." Maybe when she catches on she'll tell him to cut out the rock music, but then he can just play the Bach records. It was delightful to imagine the strains of Bach pervading the temple grounds after the priest had gone out on some errand. Bach's music was made to be heard in a temple.

Then a bit of a squabble occurred. Little sister Rie refused to part with the stereo. It seemed that Rie, who was in the habit of imitating big brother, also listened to music with the headphones, and had come to see the stereo as common property. He'd get annoyed at her for imitating him, and then she would rebel against him. Her resentment of her brother was only exacerbated by the fact that his parents had recently been indulging him and giving him things.

I explained, "Once he moves to the temple he won't be able to get such things."

Rie responded, "You'll still be able to buy stuff for him."

"No, I won't. When he goes to live at the temple, he'll become an acolyte monk. And they can't get things like stereos."

"Why not?"

Explaining to a fifth-grade girl about "leaving home to take religious vows" was not easy. I carried out the stereo as she watched with tears in her eyes. Then she stuck her hand in the bag that Ryokai was carrying out to check that none of her tapes was in there. While continuing to complain, she grabbed a couple of cassettes and hid them.

He changed into his robes, and hung his surplice and a black monk's traveling pouch around his neck. His only modern attire was his white sneakers. Then, Ryokai stood at the entrance of our home, and turned to my wife and told her, "Mother, thank you for taking care of me all this time."

"Do take good care of yourself," my wife said, disappearing into the house. I thought she would come back out to see him off, but she didn't. I let Ryokai into the passenger seat, and drove off. Ryokai left just like he always did when we were going out; he didn't even turn around to look back.

In the car, I told him about how valuable it is to face hardships when one is young. I'd told him all this the night before, but I said it again: about how I'd lost my mother when I was just his age, and how I'd left home to attend school. This was during the war against the United States. Then, after the war, I'd gone to America and, while working part time, managed to graduate from university. In spite of overcoming hardships, I wasn't really able to succeed because I had no clear goal, no good teacher, and no discipline. As I got older, I gradually came to realize these things. "You've got a definite goal, found a rare teacher, and now can live a disciplined life. Nothing could be more fortunate and auspicious than that."

My son kept looking straight ahead, so I couldn't figure out whether he was listening to me or not. Then, after a moment's silence, he suddenly spoke up. "Dad, why didn't you become a monk?"

"Well, son—" I gripped the steering wheel too tightly, and almost veered into a car in the next lane.

Getting back into my lane quickly, I continued, "The conditions were just not ripe at the time. For one thing, the times were different then. When your father was young, America was his overriding concern, you see? But now I have no such concern. Now my main concern is my own self. Everyone just thinks about themselves and acts accordingly. People who truly know how to take care of themselves, however, are rare. In Zen, one takes care of oneself—you face yourself. Keeping your own nose down to the ground is Zen."

"The priest says that, too."

"When I was young, my eyes were turned toward America." I was getting absorbed in what I was saying. "For me, America seemed to be the most fascinating place in the world. I thought that if I went there, I could discover something important. But now, my eyes are turned inward, toward myself. I can't say whether I'm really seeing myself or not, but at least I'm looking. Me, and you, too. We're really one and the same. I don't know—maybe it's because I went to America, but I feel the same way about America now. If I hadn't gone, who knows?"

"I think I'm different than you, Dad."

"We're different, alright. Understanding the difference is also part of Zen. It's said that self is not other. And yet it's also true that self is other."

I was sounding like the priest now, and it was getting hard to pay attention to the road, so I changed the subject. "You've changed quite a bit since your ordination ceremony, haven't you. When the priest asked you if you wanted to be a monk, it seems you said, 'I don't have any confidence.'" Did my son really decide on his own to become a monk? And is he satisfied with that choice? I had finally said what was on my mind.

"It's the same," he responded, blankly. "I still don't have any confidence. But, then, the priest said that nobody does from the very beginning. She said it'll come in time, though."

"Yep. It'll come in time for sure," I replied, as I gripped the steering wheel and nodded vigorously.

"She told me just to devote myself to the practice without thinking about anything else. Just practice for myself."

"Uh-huh. That's the spirit. Don't think about anything else. You are you; no need to be thinking about your mother and father. Just become a worthy monk, that's all." Warm tears welled up in my eyes.

I found myself thinking: I need not be concerned with the way things have gone so far; what's done is done; it will certainly turn out fine. It seemed as if I were trying to suppress the last remnants of doubt and uncertainty. My son turned on the radio, and, as pop music filled the car, he started drumming out the rhythm with his fingers.

When we arrived at the temple, my son put his palms on the tatami, and bowed to the priest, who was sitting at the *kotatsu** sipping tea.

"I have just returned from the Kimuras'," he announced.

She grunted, and turned to me: "Thanks for all your troubles."

* A low table with a heater built into its underside.

I was rather naive when it came to the name change. In short, I'd imagined that it was merely a matter of my son changing names, not of actually being adopted. I'd thought he was just receiving a new name; I hadn't expected that he was to become a member of that family.

Only when I heard from our ward office that the priest had petitioned the courts to have our son's name removed from the family register did I realize how serious it was.

When I got home, I blurted out to my wife, "She's going to court to have his name removed from our family register."

"Oh?" replied my wife. She didn't seem surprised. "Well, that's what has to be done in a case like this, isn't it."

I was somewhat accustomed to such unexpected replies, but her tone of voice shocked me. "You're awfully calm about this," I said.

Being a mother, maybe she'd been prepared for this ever since she'd heard about the name change. Perhaps she was not upset because we'd already been through the ceremony in which the child cuts his ties with his parents.

I had always consulted my wife about these things, but she hadn't once objected. When the ordination ceremony was over, the priest had lowered her head and told us that, in cases like these, the mother is usually opposed. "But I'm a resolute person who makes up her mind just like that," my wife later said with a laugh, when she spoke to others about it.

When our son left for the temple, and she hadn't come out to see him off, I had attributed this to her "resolute spirit." So, I was surprised to come home and see her eyes swollen. Her eyes remained blood-shot for days, only adding to the despondent mood that hung over the house. Pretending to believe in her "resolute spirit," I continued to act as if her sorrow was only a momentary impulse. I ignored it.

Now, she spoke facing the sink, with her back toward me, "I'm just doing as you said. The same as when his name was changed."

"Don't say that! Haven't we been discussing it all along?"

She was angry about something, but I didn't know what it was. Maybe she missed her son more than she had expected, and was irritated at not knowing how to handle her sorrow. "You decided everything on your own! You don't even know how I feel."

Here we go again. No matter how small the gap between us, we always seem to short circuit and end up here. I said, "I'm not talking about that. I'm talking about our son's name being removed from the family register."

"You knew it was coming to that, didn't you? It's a little late to bring it up now. You're so naive. Aren't you the one that decided this? If you're against it, you should have put a stop to it."

"You're right. But it's not that I'm naive. It's that I just keep forgetting what it really means for our son to have taken his vows."

I lost my courage when she said I should have put a stop to it. And she went on: "What are you trying to say? I hate it when you're irresolute. I don't mind so much that he's given up the Kimura name. Wasn't it you that said he's still our son? Besides, I don't particularly like the name Kimura. What the priest said to you was right: If he grows up with the name Kimura he'll definitely get into trouble with the girls, just like you."

"Wait a minute! That was when I was young, in America."

"And he's just about that age now."

When the priest and I used to chat after zazen, she would often say in that friendly voice of hers, "Ryokai's asking me, 'When will I become a Gyokusen?' And he carefully wrote in this year's schoolbooks, 'Gyokusen 'Ryokai.' Seems like he can't wait."

"Well, we'll have to take care of the paperwork right away," I would reply, trying to put off the adoption proceedings for the moment.

"When you come, he says to me, 'Mr. Kimura just arrived.' Funny kid. He should say, 'My father just arrived.' Seems to think he's already a Gyokusen."

I was a bit disappointed to hear that. But, then again, I'd expected it. He's always been resolute like his mother. It's best this way; it would do him no good to get homesick.

"Well, if that's the case I'll try to see that it's authorized as soon as possible," the middle-aged female clerk in a cardigan kindly said to my wife and me.

I wanted to say that there's really no hurry, but held back.

"We have the parents come in to make sure that they really are in agreement about it. Some people make the children work at home or elsewhere. In the

worst cases, the kids are used as security on a loan. It's really quite rare that parents give their children up for such a noble cause like you are."

I listened with some uneasiness. She must've seen hundreds of adoption cases. Probably knew all the tricks, too. It was my first experience though, and I felt helpless. Where, I wondered, is the guarantee that all will go well?

"The priest is a noble person," the words just came out. "If she weren't, we wouldn't even have considered such a thing. She's had a tough life. Mistreated by her stepmother, she ran away when she was about ten and did all kinds of work: babysitting, working in a lumberyard, a stationery store, fortunetelling, maiden at a Shinto shrine, an extra in films, scriptwriter, civil servant, you name it. She knows both sides of this world. When she buys a single piece of paper, she knows at a glance the wholesale and the retail value, as well as the quality. And she knows better than the carpenters these days about the price of wood, and how to plane it properly, how to erect a pillar, and even how to paint a wall. She knows how to do most everything in the traditional way: serve tea, pickle vegetables, prepare gift packages, and write greeting cards. It's frightening. When people visit her and ramble on without saying what they really want to, she just tells them: 'Don't you really want to talk about such and such? Come on, out with it!' She's just like those priests that parishioners used to confide in when they had problems back in the old days. And the fact that this priest's a woman makes it even more amazing. She's like a man, but has the kind of penetrating insight that only a woman could have. It's almost like she isn't human. Not the kind of person you'd want for an enemy! But on your side, she's someone you can really rely on."

I glanced up at the clerk, seeking encouragement.

"How old is this priest?" she asked quietly.

"Well, I'm not sure. I suppose around sixty-five or sixty-six."

"And how's her health?"

"Her health?" I repeated, startled by the question. "Actually, it's not so good. She's had liver surgery. She seems to continue by sheer willpower. I do hope she stays well until my son completes his training."

"It does seem that people who train hard when they're young tend to become easily incapacitated in old age. Does she have any relatives?"

"I've heard she has some in the Hokuriku region. But, then, she's changed her name, and she left there so many years ago . . ."

"In that case, your son is the sole relative, isn't he?"

"I guess so," I replied, startled again.

"You'd better think about that, although I assume you already have."

"About . . . what?"

"The person she adopts is responsible for her support."

"Indeed," I gulped. "Yes, well, I realize that."

"It's important," she continued. "Why, just the other day, the real parent of a child adopted by a priest killed the priest for breach of contract. It was an extreme case, but the priest had concealed an illness, and that seems to have been a contributing factor. And you never know what will happen, even with healthy people."

"That's true. But this priest puts the training first. She's the type that would tell you to do zazen even when one of your parents passes away."

"I was just telling you these things happen, that's all," the clerk smiled.

"He won't be back in your house for three years," the priest told me, soon after Ryokai's name had been removed from our family register. "He's got to be weaned from all the worldly habits and indulgences he's grown up with. You've been spoiling him recently, haven't you? After three years, I'll see. Might take longer—who knows?"

Returning home, I reported this to my wife.

"It's hopeless," she sighed. Then she said, "She won't let him come home even after three years. I know it. Who was it who'd said he'd come home every Saturday? Now he won't even be home for the new year. And I wanted to take him to a hot springs resort. The boy loves hot springs. The pleasures in my life are getting fewer and fewer. When I do what you say, things just get all screwed up. It's no problem for you, though—you can see him on Sundays."

"If you want to see him, why don't you just go to the temple? There are a number of annual ceremonies and services."

"I'm not going to start participating in that stuff all of a sudden just because I want to see my son. I won't be seen stooping to that level."

The desk and chair she had been saving for him to use were now given to Rie, and all his books and things in the desk were stuffed in a closet. My wife now tended to remain silent even during meals; cleaning up the dishes or hanging the clothes to dry, she would hum to herself. Sometimes, she would stand out on the veranda, staring at the road that led to the train station. It was the road our son always took to school. Adjusting his cap as it slid down his shaven head, he pedaled his bicycle along the tree-lined street until he disappeared behind the hill to the left.

As I approach, I can hear her humming quietly "Jesu Joy of Man's Desiring," the piece our son had loved. He used to sound it out on the piano keys with his index fingers. The record was put away after our son left; once, I tried to play it, but my wife asked me to turn it off.

I stand by her without saying a word. Without turning to look at me, she just continues staring into space. Sometimes she speaks up. "It feels like Ryota will appear any minute from out of those trees over there, his white head like an egg, bobbing up and down."

She doesn't call him Ryokai anymore. Even if I say Ryokai, she stubbornly responds with Ryota. At the dinner table, she serves the hamburger that he loved, saying, "If Ryota were here, he'd say, 'Wow, my favorite!'"

He was an adorable kid. Whatever it was, he couldn't keep quiet about it. What kind of monk will he be? I couldn't help but wonder if maybe the life of a chatty, tea-serving priest would suit him. He sure liked to joke around.

"I pigged out on a hamburger at school today. My teacher gave it to me."

"You begged him for it, didn't you. You shouldn't have," my wife responds in all seriousness.

"Just kidding!" he laughs.

He often pulled the same kinds of tricks on Rie, then burst out laughing. She, too, took him seriously, then, when she realized she had been fooled, she would hit him with a nearby pillow or doll.

Ryota rarely played with Rie, except when he was teasing her. But Rie would spy on her big brother and imitate whatever he was doing. She'd draw the same pictures, listen to the same music, watch the same TV programs. Rie's affection for her brother was a one-way street, though. They were always arguing over color markers or cassette tapes. The quarreling never seemed to stop, except when they were sitting in front of the TV or the stereo. Only then did I feel they were indeed siblings.

Rie's companion is gone, so she gets bored, discouraged, and lonely.

"When he was here he was always teasing you," I offer.

"I still liked it better when he was here," she answers.

It really got to me when Rie looked lonely like that. I realized I had been forgetting her feelings. Preoccupied with Ryota, I failed to see the adverse effect it was having on the rest of the family. It is Rie more than Ryota who is filled with love for people and animals. From the standpoint of aptitude, Rie may be more suited for the priesthood than Ryota. I came to worry more about Rie's being deeply hurt because of her sensitive feelings.

On Sundays, I got into the habit of dispensing tidbits of information about Ryokai as the family sat around the dinner table. But, even this news I heard not firsthand, but from the priest or the woman who helped around the temple. The priest had forbidden me to speak directly with him.

"The parents hamper the training more than anything else," she had told me.

She's certainly right about that, I thought. Parents want to approach their kids whenever the opportunity arises, and give them spending money or treats.

"Absolutely no more giving him spending money," she said. "All of his needs will be taken care of by the temple. We all get a salary, just like in a company. I receive twenty thousand yen each month. Ryokai will also start getting paid soon enough. So, don't give him money on the sly. If you've got something to give to him, tell me about it. Don't ever give anything directly to him."

Thus, all direct contact was stopped. All I could do was watch from a distance as he swept the garden, wiped the floors, or did zazen. During meals I sat on one side, and he on the other, with the priest in the middle. It felt like we had been transported to another country, full of strict regulations.

When we happened to pass by each other as we cleaned up after a meal or did other work, I would whisper furtively, "Hey, how's it goin'?"

"Fine," was all he'd say, with a strained expression on his face and eyes casting about. He didn't seem like my son anymore, which made me feel irritated, and miserable. I never saw him having the least bit of fun, messing around like he did at home. Was there a place where he could do that now? I worried about whether he would be able to stand the stress he was under.

My wife made some of his favorite food, and asked me to take it to him, but I told her we had been warned once already and should let sleeping dogs lie. If we were to take such things, it would have to be for the temple, but we couldn't give leftovers to the temple. And if we went and bought his favorite meat, it would be even more obvious, wouldn't it?

Even the New Year's gift of money, which his grandparents gave him every year, was returned. "Give it back, and tell them please not to do such a thing again."

Well, I tried, but you can't very well give back a New Year's gift. We decided to deposit the money into a bank account in my son's name, but I wonder when we'll be able to give it to him.

The priest had told me to bear with it no matter how cruel it may look, but now I realize that was not for the benefit of my son. It was for the parents.

Ryokai's parents had to stay away from him, but not so his other "parent." That is, the new "parishioner parent."

"I've thought it over and decided on the head of the parish association," the priest told me. He was the owner of the market in front of the train station. When his wife was deathly ill with tetanus, he would purify his body every morning before work, and come to offer prayers at the temple. One morning, I happened to see him crying as he made supplications in front of the statue of Shakyamuni Buddha in the main hall. His wife escaped death by a miracle.

During the gathering after Ryokai's ordination ceremony, he had raised his glass for a toast and, with tears in his eyes, grasped my hand and said, "Now the temple will be all right. It will be safe."

"Well, he's easily moved to tears, but there's no one more pious," the priest had once told me.

A "parishioner parent" seems to be someone that a monk in training can go to talk to about things he can't speak about with his priest. In the event that the priest passes away, the parishioner parent takes care of the monk in place of the real parents. "In an emergency, the real parents are useless," the priest said.

Even if the priest dies, then, we won't be the ones to take care of him.

"I suppose you already know, but sons rebel against their parents, and seldom seek out their advice. Small children and hopelessly dependent people are exceptions, of course."

This parishioner parent brings Ryokai all kinds of things. And the priest is delighted about it. "What should I bring him next time?" he asks the priest.

"Let's see. He hasn't had any meat lately, so bring him some of that," the priest replies.

"OK," he says. Then, with a giant plate of sukiyaki meat from his market, he brings his wife and children for a barbecue under a cherry tree in front of the main hall.

During the midsummer's and New Year's festivities, he brings shirts, underwear, and such, "for Ryokai."

"He brings stuff for Ryokai, but nothing for me," the priest says, although she doesn't seem upset about it.

The priest enjoys talking to people about Ryokai. She's generally fond of gossip and small talk—a feminine trait difficult to eradicate, it seems— although it does allow us to know how our son is getting along. Especially about school, we have no way of knowing, except from the priest. Well, the woman who helps out around the temple sometimes keeps me informed, whispering in my ear by the kitchen door.

"How did he do in his last test?"—when I would ask the priest about such things, she would suddenly get cross. "Don't be deceived by such minor things. If you worry about every point he gains or loses, there's no end to it. What's so important about grades? I've told Ryokai: As long as you pass, it's all right. I'm usually not very fond of those who excel in school. Maybe it's a rotten thing to say to a scholar like yourself, but scholars are not good for much. Always thinking about trivial things, they're a timid lot. You won't get anywhere just by thinking. Ryokai has inherited a bit of your nervous disposition, and that'll have to be corrected. I don't ask about his scores after every test."

I should have known that asking her about his grades would be like the koan of taking the golden bell from around the lion's neck.

But then his grades started improving. The woman helper whispered in my ears: "Eleventh in his class this time; three up from last time. Doing well in English, but math and science still no good. Perfect score in religion classes."

Another time, she offered, "Eighth from the top now. Improved by three again. His scores in math have gone up eight points. Ryokai's studying hard."

The woman helper told me these things as if the priest would be after her with the kyosaku if she found out.

Considering how he'd been second or third from the bottom in the previous school, this was quite a change. The priest had told Ryokai not to worry about his grades, but she also told him to do his best in math and calligraphy. They're essential for running the temple. That's why she made him keep track of every cent in his account book. Calligraphy is useful for writing out the wooden strips for graves. Since Ryokai was left-handed, his calligraphy looked kind of like matchstick men. It seemed to me it would be difficult to correct. My son had never even given a thought to penmanship, but one word from the priest, and he joined the calligraphy club at school, and switched to writing with his right hand. His work was eventually displayed not only in school, but in other exhibitions as well, and it even won some prizes. The power of that priest is awesome.

During a chat with the priest over tea, I asked, "What prizes did he receive?"

"What? Oh, something from the temple headquarters. Better not win anymore; he'll get a big head."

Then she changed the topic. "He's got to apply himself more to math. He hasn't even gotten the fundamentals down yet."

"Perhaps that's because I hated math," I offered.

"He's doing well in English, like you the English-teacher, but he doesn't have a firm grasp of the basic sentence patterns. What were his parents doing? Maybe he can get a good grade in English just by memorizing, but math doesn't work that way. He's got to be able to apply it. He's too rigid, like you. When he does one thing, he forgets everything else. Like father, like son. Oh, he's earnest, all right. And he'll get better; he's still young. But I've told him not to worry about English, to concentrate on math instead. The other day, he got a ninety-eight on an English test. I didn't say one word, so he asked me why I didn't compliment him for it. I told him not to speak such nonsense. Is English necessary for a monk? Do you want to go abroad and give Zen talks? Sure, some priests do, but I think it's despicable. English is of no use for a monk undergoing strict Zen training. That's what I told him."

My son got the point. When his homeroom teacher recommended him for a special English class, he declined. (To improve the chances for students to get into better universities, my son's school had set up special classes to improve English and math education. It was an honor to be selected for such a class.)

"Seems the teacher was left with his mouth wide open when Ryokai told him that he wasn't interested because his Zen master'd said all he has to do is get a passing grade!" the priest laughed.

I heard his homeroom teacher had also recommended him as class representative, but he declined that as well, saying his master dislikes such things.

"Why can't we see his report card?" asked my wife.

"It's not like we're giving him gifts or money. We just want to see it. What's so bad about parents knowing their children's grades?"

"But we're no longer his parents," I said, almost overwhelmed by the weight of my own words.

"What are you saying! I gave birth to that boy. And I can never forget the pain I suffered in doing so. How could that woman understand?"

This was the first time I had ever heard my wife call the priest "that woman."

"It's a different issue. He's entered the Buddhist priesthood. Now it's not his parents' teaching that he follows but the Buddha's."

"You mean the priest's teaching. Anyway, I know that. Ever since he had his head shaved at the ordination ceremony, I've known he was taking a different path than ours. That's why I just watched without saying a word. I've tried not to interfere so far, and intend to continue that way. But what's wrong with us knowing what he's doing? Other people know. It's not something that needs to be kept secret, is it? Why is it that only the parents are kept in the dark?"

I had no answer for her. We had no right as parents to know? That seemed to be the priest's reasoning. She called it the "parental blind spot." Thinking that way, she must really have looked down on us. Yet, we had to think about the same things that she did. We'd had to have his name removed from our register so that she could adopt him. Now our son was in her hands, and with our blessings. The least she could do, out of common courtesy, was keep us informed. It's not as if we were going to get up in arms after hearing things about him. We just couldn't think of him as a stranger. Our feelings for him can't be changed as long as we live. Even though we give up all our parental desires, our feelings for him remain. Is this just a "parental blind spot"?

And what about the priest? Has she no blind spot? When she treats Ryokai with love, is there no "parental feeling"? It is because we see her treat Ryokai with love that we are so thankful as to put our palms together in prayer. We never feel envy or bitterness towards her. All parents are filled with delight at seeing their children treated with love. Why, then, does she not understand the feelings of us, his own parents?

Ryokai's being made heir is no doubt deeply connected with the priest's lifelong desire to restore Zenkaiji Temple. In the confusion of the postwar land reform, she held onto over ten thousand square meters of temple land, and rebuilt the main hall and living quarters, which had been reduced to run-down, leaky thatch huts, into magnificent structures with roofs of copper and tile. Not only that, but she had other buildings erected: an annex for guests, dorm rooms for monks, and a pagoda to house the Buddhist scriptures. She constructed landscape gardens around the grounds, remembering to include flowers for each of the seasons. If the priest had been born in the Kamakura era rather than in the present decadent one, she probably would have presided over an enormous monastic complex with many temples around the country.

Anyway, with the construction and restoration completed, next a successor is needed. Ryokai's appearance was, without doubt, the final and finishing touch. And that was fine with me. My wife and I had no objections to that. Perhaps the priest would say it was for the prosperity of Buddhism. But did this all have nothing to do with the priest's own personal ambitions? What exactly was the connection between the enthusiastic temple construction and her own peculiar monkish philosophy? Why the imposing monastery layout? Wouldn't Ryokai's "religious training" end up being little more than maintaining and developing this enormous religious estate? In short, wouldn't he be no more than a puppet for the priest's ambitions? It would be fine if he could maintain and develop it, but if he couldn't, then he might end up drowning in ten thousand square meters of temple management.

When I got all upset thinking about this, my wife told me, "You're not able to say anything to the priest's face. I'm right, aren't I."

"What should I say?"

"You should ask what our son is doing. But, really, you don't know how to ask, do you. What you tell me is often quite different from what happens. I thought he'd be home on Saturdays, and at least once a year be able to take a vacation with us. Now we can't even find out what his grades are. Why didn't we know from the beginning it would be like this?"

"Okay, okay. But how was I supposed to know? I've never been a monk."

"Do you know what everyone is saying?" My wife looked up at me as she spoke. "My friends, I mean, and people who've met you. They all say you and I are taken advantage of, used by others. They say we're ignorant of the ways of the world."

"They're sure right about that—we're ignorant of the world, all right."

"They say all the temples are in trouble because they have no successors. I heard a priest had put an ad in the local paper saying that he would give his daughter and even pay educational expenses. When I tell people that we gave up our son and now he can't even return home for three years, they're just astonished."

"But Ryota himself wanted to leave home to take religious vows." I said Ryota without thinking.

"I wonder whether it really was his wish."

I remained silent.

"I'd like to ask him next chance I get. I've been kept in the dark so long. It seems like you and the priest discussed it, then Ryota just disappeared from my life before I knew it."

I said, "He's the one who first mentioned it. No doubt about it. I can still remember the serious look in his eyes. Sure, he wavered a bit, but he never lost the desire to be a monk. If we had just let it be, he might have lost interest. Maybe that's what we should have done. Who knows? But no, he couldn't have lost interest. The desire would have lay buried deep inside. Then, when he got older, he would have regretted not having become a monk. I'm sure of it: it was decided a long time ago. There are a number of guys like that coming to the zazen gatherings. One of them was given up for adoption when he was young, so he couldn't become a monk. Now he's working hard so that when his son is old enough, the father will close down his business and become a monk no matter what anyone says. It's never too late, but if you're going to do it anyway, the sooner the better. To be a real monk you've got to see into hundreds of koan. But, if you start too late, you'll pass away before you've seen through ten or twenty."

"You always persuade me by talking that kind of nonsense. Whatever it is, I end up having to agree with you. And that's exactly why I need you to take a stand. If the priest won't talk to you about it, why don't you ask Ryota directly?" my wife said, looking me right in the eye. "I mean, we can't even talk to our own son?"

"Sure doesn't seem right," I said, then felt my cheeks quiver as I tried to force a smile.

The first time my wife saw our son after he left home was at the school festival. The woman who helped out at the temple told me what day it was to be held. Our son was now going to high school at the same institution. Since we had always gone to the festivals when he was in junior high, this chance to continue the tradition was certainly a comfort to my wife. With our daughter in tow, we set out. We went to his homeroom, but he wasn't there. When we asked a classmate where we might find him, we were told he could be found in the school's Zen meditation hall, where he was in charge of an exhibition of Buddhist paintings and calligraphy.

As we approached the meditation hall, the door was open, and there, in the back, was our son. He was standing before some scrolls on the wall, talking to a young man with a necktie and close-cropped hair.

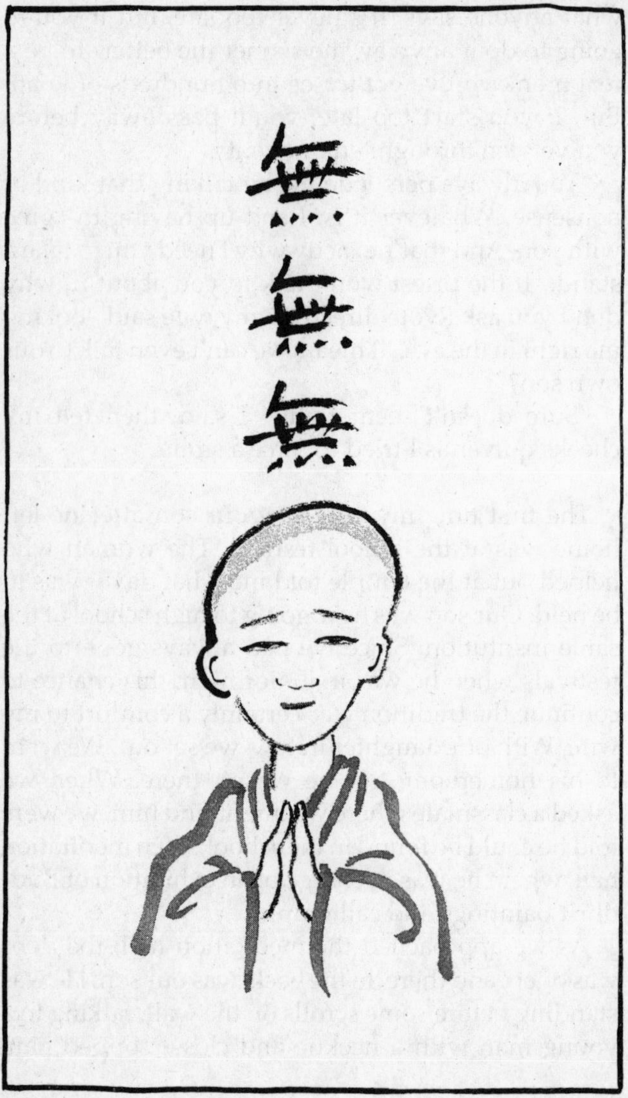
無
無
無

My wife stopped at the entrance, not wanting to go in. It felt as if we were waiting for special permission to enter a hall of national treasures.

"What're you waiting for? Hurry up, let's go in," Rie coaxed my wife until she entered, timidly.

My son was still talking, but soon noticed us, and nodded hello without much change of expression. He continued to converse with his companion.

We walked around a bit, looking at the exhibit. Although my wife was not interested in such things, she pretended to be.

"Let's go over to him," Rie said as she pulled on her mother's hand.

"Not yet. Can't you see he's talking with someone?" she answered, walking slowly.

He soon finished talking, bowed to the young teacher, then disappeared.

"Mom, he's gone." Rie said.

"Oh, really?" my wife responded, then looking somewhat relieved said, "Well, he must be very busy."

"It looks like he doesn't want to see us," Rie spoke with a resentful tone. "At least he could've come and said hello."

"Well," my wife said with a saddened air, "maybe he doesn't care about us anymore."

Trying to comfort her, I said, "Boys are like that. They never think about their parents as much as their parents would like. And if they did, why we wouldn't know what to do. I know—I used to be like that too."

But my wife just turned away without a word.

The second chance for my wife to see him was on the Buddhist All Souls' Day, a midsummer memorial service at the temple. Since this was an annual service we all had attended before, my wife felt it natural to attend this year as well.

Forty-nine large, colored strips of paper in honor of the deceased were hanging down from the lintels surrounding the main hall, and bamboo decorated the two main pillars. The strips of colored paper flapped, and the bamboo leaves rustled in the heat of the summer wind, giving a momentary lightness to the darkened hall, and producing a sound like a cool, refreshing breeze.

The memorial service began with sutra chanting. The priest, sporting a gorgeous golden surplice and bulky robes, with only her head popping out, droned the sutras with a disinterested look. The accompanying monk was Ryokai. Sitting off to the side in the shade of the Buddhist altar, he beat out the time on a large piece of round wood shaped like a fish, occasionally striking a bowl-shaped gong. My wife's eyes turned red; she dabbed at them with her handkerchief as she looked at him in his robes and rather strained countenance. Next to her was Rie, legs half folded under her, fidgeting occasionally.

"Ryota's no good at that, is he, Mom?" Rie says as she looks up at her, but mother is too preoccupied with her own thoughts to answer.

I had also been thinking that his drumming was rather poor. Getting stronger, then slackening, even getting off the beat. At first I thought it was because he was new at it, but there was something else. Then I realized it: He was beating time like he had when he'd played drums in the school band. A smile played across my lips as I thought of it.

When the sutra chanting was finished, the priest virtually leapt up onto the gold-leaf lecture chair, folded her legs under her, and gave her annual All Souls' Day lecture about the Buddhist Saint Mokuren and his mother. This saint possessed the most marvelous powers, and was eager to save his mother, who had fallen into the hell of hunger and thirst.

"So, there are monks concerned about their mothers," my wife whispered to me.

I remained silent as I watched the priest wipe the sweat from her brow with a towel. She must have been hot as hell, wrapped up in all those robes. Her faltering yet frank way of speaking had a certain appeal, but once she digressed from the main subject, it took a while for her to return. Each year, the story changed a little; this time she added a part about the deep sinfulness of women.

"It's said that women by nature are guilty of seven deadly sins. Thus, it requires tremendous effort for a woman to be saved. Mokuren's mother was an extremely greedy person, but she's not the only one to fall into this hell of hunger and thirst. Who knows when any of you will fall. Nay, maybe you've already fallen."

Saying this, the priest looked around at the audience. Most of them were middle-aged women, and lots of elderly people, too. One of them, who looked like she had elephantiasis, had her legs extended and out to one side as she turned and talked to the person next to her.

"Shakyamuni Buddha said that, in one day, man transmigrates through the six hellish paths of existence. Do you know these six hellish paths? They are the hells of pain, hunger and thirst, beasts, incessant fighting, the human realm, and the celestial realm. Human beings are going round and round in these six realms of existence. In a single day we fall how many times into the hell of pain, the hell of hunger and thirst, the hell of beasts.

"And you don't fall into these hells just when you do something bad, either. Whenever you doubt someone, feel jealous, get carried away by your delusions, or become angry, you're falling into the hell of hunger and thirst, or the hell of pain. Hey, tofu maker!" the priest yelled at the old woman who was talking to her neighbor.

"Can't you keep quiet? If you want to talk, go out and do it, all right? Reckless jabbering like that breaks the precept against improper speech, you know. That's a great way to end up in the hell of hunger and thirst."

The elderly tofu maker turned to her companion: "Whad'd she just say?" and cocked her ear. Hard of hearing.

"A person's mind and heart are dirty things," said the priest, returning to her lecture. "You know the expression 'The mind of a horse and the heart of a monkey.' What you're thinking about changes just like that. All of you, take a good look inside yourselves and see. Changing all the time. Especially women. That's why women aren't suited for religious practice. Worse yet, they try to conceal their fickleness.

"I have a special talent for seeing into people's hearts. Don't use it much anymore, but I used to look into people's hearts with it often enough. Once, a couple of ladies came to see me and they told me they had been talking about such and such on the way here. I told them not to lie, that they really had been discussing so and so. Boy, were they surprised. They wondered how the heck I knew. Gradually, this ability became a bother, so I gave it up. I don't need to do it; the Buddha can see it all. Better not forget about the Buddha. That's my lecture for today." The priest then seemed absorbed in chanting something to herself as she placed her palms together.

Following this, some long folding tables were brought into the main hall, and we were treated to the chilled noodles, vegetables, and fruits that the women had prepared. The parishioners were grocers, tofu makers, noodle-shop owners, and the like, so the food was fresh, and there was plenty of it.

Ryokai tied back the wide sleeves of his robe and walked around the tables. Women were serving the food, but when something else needed to be done he was always asked, so he seemed quite busy. Also, he was quite popular, often being asked by the others to sit down and have a bite to eat.

The three of us sat in a corner, moving chopsticks to our lips and watching from a distance.

Soon Rie finished her meal and went off somewhere to play; my wife and I were just finishing ours when we heard someone call out from the other side of the table: "Mr. Kimura, Mr. Kimura."

It was Mr. Ota, owner of the market, head of the parish association, and Ryokai's parishioner parent. He was calling us over. "Don't sit off in a corner. Come on over here! Ryokai's here, too. Why don't you come over and talk with us?"

Ryokai had been stopped by Mr. Ota and was sitting next to him, eating something that his parishioner parent had given him and smiling as he answered something. Mr. Ota probably thought it was rude to keep Ryokai all to himself right in the presence of his real parents. Standing, the stooped Mr. Ota tottered over to us. "Come on, it's all right. Why don't you join us? Ryokai's really turned out well. He'll make a fine priest. Why, he's my pride and joy. Nothing like that useless, rascal son of mine. I'm always telling him he should be like Ryokai. I really do think of him as my own son. It's an honor, that's what it is. It's all the Buddha's doing. Come on, come on! You're the real parents, aren't you? No need to hesitate—"

"Why don't you keep your mouth shut!" The priest's voice suddenly rose from behind Mr. Ota.

She was sitting at another table, talking with some female parishioners. She always seemed to have one eye on Ryokai, and Mr. Ota's voice had been getting louder. She continued, "Just let it be. Going on like that, you grate on my nerves. You're the parent. You and I are Ryokai's only parents now."

Mr. Ota seemed lost in space for a moment, no idea what to do, troubled and embarrassed. With a pathetic smile, he started mumbling, "Well, I'll be going now . . . Uh, see you again later . . ." Stooped over, he turned and went back to where he had been sitting.

Taking a mouthful of now stale tea, I turned to my wife and said, "Let's go home."

Without answering me, she looked around and wondered aloud, "Where did Rie run off to?"

Just then, Rie appeared from the far hallway, clutching something in her hand, and with a delighted look on her face. "Where did you go? To the bathroom?" my wife said, with a sense of relief.

"I went to see my brother's room. The stereo was there, everything." "Idiot!" I exclaimed. "You shouldn't have done that."

"But it was my stereo, too," she pouted. "Look!" She showed us what she had in her hand. "This is my tape. I wondered what had happened to it. Ryota took it all right."

"How could you take back such a thing?" I said.

"Because it's mine, and I'll tell him so."

"No, you needn't tell him."

"I think you should tell him," said my wife, taking our daughter's side.

"It'll bother him if things just disappear when he's not around."

"But—"

Then, I caught a glimpse of the priest, who was wrapped up in conversation with one of the local parishioners. My wife spoke: "Why can't she tell him? Rie can't even talk to him about this? There's nothing wrong with that, is there? Do we have a disease like typhoid or something? Is this the reward I get for bringing him into the world? Is this how we're treated for allowing him to come live here?"

Surprised at her mother's angry look, Rie stood up.

"Go. Go and tell your brother that you're taking it home."

Rie cut through the tables of food and went to where her brother was seated. Standing there, she showed him the cassette tape and said something.

Ryokai, stretched out his hand and rose up as if to grab it.

"It's mine!" Rie screamed.

"No, it's not. I recorded on it, just the other day. I taped over what was on it."

"How could you! You recorded over my tape. It's mine."

Ryokai had no money to buy a new one, so he'd used Rie's.

"What's going on!" the priest yelled. "This is no place for such foolishness."

Ryokai explained to the priest how Rie was trying to take the tape on which he had recorded some music from a radio program.

The priest yelled again: "Give it to her! Give her whatever she wants. If a monk gets attached to such a thing, what will become of him? A monk's music is sutra recitation. Don't you understand what I've been talking about?"

Ryokai sat down with a pale face.

We put some dumplings and fruit in a plastic bag to take home, got up, went to the entrance of the main hall, bowed, and were about to leave when the priest approached.

"I have something I want to say to you." She stood there. "I understand how you feel about Ryokai, but it just disturbs him. Parents' feelings disturb religious training more than anything else, because when a child begins religious training, the emotional ties between parent and child are the most difficult thing to cut. I don't want him to be half-assed like you. If 'half-assed' is not a proper word, then let's call it lacking stability, lacking composure.

"Long ago, in Tang dynasty China, there was a priest named Tozan Ryokai, one of the spiritual fore-fathers of our Soto branch of Zen Buddhism. He had a deep sense of filial piety, and often sent all kinds of things from the temple to his parents in the country-side. He didn't go to visit them, although his parents would sometimes visit the temple to pray and listen to their son's sermons. Then, one day, his father died. His mother, now alone, packed up her things, and headed for the temple, thinking she would be taken care of by her son, the priest. When she arrived and told him this, Priest Tozan said it was impossible. He tried his best to explain why he could not do this, but his mother just could not comprehend. Finally, he had one of his senior monks take his mother and her baggage out of the temple. His mother pleaded over and over outside the temple gate to be let back in, but the gate was kept tightly shut and she never set foot in the temple again. Her face streaming with tears, she finally returned home. After that, she went back to the temple a number of times, but Priest Tozan refused to meet with her.

"See what I mean? That's how rigorous our reli-gious practice must be. Remember this story, and consider it well."

"If only our son turns into a fine human being, that's what counts. It doesn't matter how we feel," I said to my wife after we returned home and were alone.

She responded, "I've already accepted that. He's not coming home again. Rie's all I have left now, so don't take her away from me. Being married to you, my pleasures in life gradually diminish."

"Take her away—what are you saying? Haven't we discussed everything and worked together? But, then again, it seems somehow like it was all destined to turn out this way from the very beginning. That's the way I see it. It's fate. Not something we could have calculated. It's a strange twist of fate, how this all began with my taking him along to the temple. And it wasn't my idea; you were the one who asked me to take him along because you had so many things to do at home."

"What!" my wife raised her voice. "You blame everything on other people—that's a bad habit of yours, you know. You always attribute things to fate or whatnot, but I think it was really your doing more than anything else. How dare you make it sound like all I wanted to do was get him out of my hair. That's the cruelest thing you could possibly say. You have no idea how I feel. I've suffered every day since Ryota left us, but you never offered one word to console me. Rie knew my sadness and would say to me, 'Mom, don't cry.' You, you never even noticed, did you. All you thought was that I just wanted to get him out of my hair, didn't you."

"No, I just thought that you would understand in time, that's all." (So, that's it. I should have said something to her then.)

"That's the kind of person you are. As long as you understand, it's all right. Others, well, they'll 'understand in time.' Tell me, just what is it that I'm supposed to understand?"

"His religious practice! If only he can do that and become a fine monk, then everything else will be solved. That's the one and only concern."

"You're always going on about his religious practice, but why do you want to make him do such a thing in the first place? You speak as if he were born to do it, but isn't it really you who wants him to do it? He wanted to play drums in the school band, but you made him take up those wooden fish and gongs. I think the one who really should do this religious practice is you, not him."

So this is what is called woman's intuition. Shocked, I could only stare into her flushed face.

"I'll tell him someday: It's your father that is most in need of religious practice. It's preposterous how you played around all you wanted, then go and make your son do this practice."

"But don't you see, that was a kind of practice too. Traveling through foreign countries when I was young was a practice of sorts. There's not a thing in this world that is not a practice we can learn from. That's something I understood only after having begun Zen practice. Everything we do is a kind of practice: walking, eating, standing, sitting."

I shut my mouth. Here I am saying the same thing to my wife that I said to those two young Americans twenty years ago in New York, minus the finger pointing. The only difference is that back then I was kidding; now, I'm serious. I went on in spite of myself.

"Even when I was playing, I was serious. I didn't know whether what I was doing was just for fun, or ascetic practice. I just couldn't help doing it. And it's no different now. Some people can just breeze through life, at ease whether they're playing or working. But I don't have that knack. And I didn't have a good teacher to guide me. Compared with me, Ryokai is—"

"Don't go blaming it on your not having a good teacher. Whenever you fail at something you blame it on someone else, or on fate. That's why the priest calls you half-assed."

Seeming to recall the time the priest said that, my wife giggled, then settled down a bit. "I think it's good if Ryota practices and becomes a fine priest. I have no intention of clinging on to him till I die, like that saint what's-his-name's mother. The priest seems to think all mothers are like that, but I'm not. That's why I won't knock myself out to go see him."

She seemed to be gradually calming down. "But I don't have a dream like you do. I've had enough of my dreams shattered—that's been the pattern from the time we got married, all the way up to now. He's no longer our son, so if I held onto a dream about him it wouldn't mean anything, anyway. If he practices and goes on to become a fine priest, that's OK with me. And if he gets tired of it, gives up, and does something else, that's OK, too. But, I would like to help him at that point. That's all I'm concerned about. I don't think that he absolutely must become a monk no matter what."

I said, "No, we must hold onto our dreams. Otherwise we have no rationale for our struggle and suffering. I don't mean unrealistic dreams like becoming an astronaut or bending spoons through mind power. I mean dreams that expand our reality, that challenge us to do tomorrow what we could not do today. It's how people improve, bit by bit."

My wife responded, "But we don't know what tomorrow will bring. I've seen many things in my life come to pass, and yet nothing's ever been the way I expected it. So I don't even think much about my future anymore. How much less do we know what will become of our son, and what will become of the temple. And the priest, she's old, and not well. What will happen if she dies? Then, I guess, he'll have to take care of the temple, and he won't be able to do that religious practice. The temple's just too big for him to handle by himself. She made it what it was. She could do it. As soon as he takes it over, maybe he'll just divide up the land and sell it off."

That Sunday, after zazen was over and I was preparing to go home, the priest appeared at the entrance of the main hall, handed me a familiar-looking plastic bag, and said, "I think you forgot this the other day." It was the bag with the dumplings and peaches in it.

After the priest had stopped me and given me a good talking to, I had completely forgotten about it. It was even fuller than before. "Put what was left in," the priest said.

"It's been awfully hot lately, and I might have been on edge, spoken too harshly, though I don't think I said anything wrong. That story about Priest Tozan, did you understand it? You can consider it a koan. In the vast heavens and throughout the earth, there's nothing that is not a koan. The child's suffering is a koan for the parent. Your son's problems are a great koan for you. You should be deeply thankful for it."

"Yes, I am," I replied agreeably, then took the conversation a step further:

"I understand perfectly that my son is now living in a different world; I intend to be on my guard so as not to forget again. From now on, our one and only desire is that our son be able to fully do his practice. Since he's become a monk, I want him to continue his practice whatever happens. But, if all he does is take care of the temple and the parishioners, then I don't know why he's here." I emphasized the last sentence.

"Uh-huh," the priest's face turned harsh for a split second, but she soon replied, "I see what you mean. I can understand right away what you want to say, 'cause I've thought about it a lot more than you have. You wonder how important the management of this temple is to me. And you worry that Ryokai's being forced into it and won't be able to do his practice. Listen up: Caring for the temple and the parishioners is important for a monk. It's also a part of his practice. Simply forgetting the world is not true religious practice. An old hermit in ancient China was criticized for getting stuck in a state he expressed as: 'A withered tree hugs a frozen crag; not a bit of warmth during the long winter.' Such practice is 'withered-tree Zen,' not living. You know that much, right?

"My concern with temple management is no mere extravagance. If I wanted that, I'd build a parking lot to rent out, or run a preschool on the grounds. I came to this temple because my master told me to. He told me to take this broken-down old temple and fix it up real nice. And it wasn't just because he told me to, either. First of all, it's for the Buddha. The finer the temple becomes, the brighter Shakyamuni Buddha's light shines. I could do nothing without Shakyamuni Buddha's power.

"Still, a temple's just a temple. Just a building. Since it's you, I'll say this, something I've never told another soul: I'll be leaving this temple eventually. I mean, after Ryokai finishes school, completes his training, and returns here. Then, I'll become a simple, wandering monk once more. Of course, I'll be too old to do any real training, but I intend to find a little hermitage in the countryside and live there. When my master left me this temple, my hope was to spend the rest of my life practicing here. But when it's time to die, I want to die a simple monk.

"I've thought about Ryokai too, and I've no intention to force this temple on him. If a monk has his own temple though, it gives him a sense of security, it's convenient, for many reasons. But if this temple gets in the way of his practice, well then he can just up and leave. I intend to tell him that too. If he staked his life on his practice, a temple would just get in the way. That's up to him."

I bowed my head.

"But," the priest changed her tone, "that's neither here nor there. It's nothing but people's dimwitted calculations. Being free from such thoughts is the best. It all just depends on the Buddha."

I wondered if she could go back to being a wandering monk so easily. Being old, her legs and back must be weak. And if she became ill, she'd need someone to take care of her. Would she really return to the life of a wandering monk, or was she just saying that?

I kept these doubts to myself, though. "Is it just a matter of Mu?" I asked

"Yep, but it's not just Mu. It's the Mu of Master Joshu when the monk asked him if a dog has the Buddha nature or not. It's the whole universe being nothing but Mu. The seer, the seeing, and the seen are all Mu."

Leaving the main hall and approaching the main gate of the temple I ran into Ryokai, who was collecting the sweepings that had been left in piles from the morning cleaning. Wrapped around his head was a small towel to ward off the summer sun. His old work clothes were too small, and out stuck his slender, white feet in worn-out straw sandals. He seemed to be brooding over something as he moved the bamboo broom. As usual, there was no change in his expression, even when someone passed nearby. This is the way Zen practitioners are supposed to act, so I wasn't really surprised, but the moment impressed me deeply, and I stopped.

In the paper bag, I was carrying some new cassette tapes. After having hesitated a number of times that morning, I'd finally decided to bring them. Rie had taken hers back, and he probably had no money to buy new ones. I didn't know whether I'd have a chance to give them to him, but I figured if I didn't I'd just bring them back home. Involved in talking with the priest I'd completely forgotten, but here and now was my chance.

I looked behind me. Through the pine branches the closed doors of the main hall were visible. Under the afternoon sun, it stood alone in dark and still silence, as if some terrible secret were contained inside of it.

"Ryokai," I called cautiously.

"Yes?" He looked at me suspiciously, then quickly turned his eyes toward the main hall.

"Here," I took the pack of cassette tapes out of the paper bag. "You don't have any, right?"

Ryokai stood there holding the bamboo broom, and turned his eyes to the modern design on the package sparkling in the sunlight. He seemed a bit dazzled by the brightness, but then looked at me and said, "Don't want 'em."

I had a sneaking suspicion he might say that, so I wasn't surprised. But I couldn't back down now, so I stood there holding the tapes.

Then he asked, "Didn't the master say anything?"

"About what?"

"That day, after the memorial service, the master told me to sit in the main hall. She did, too. No dinner; we sat through till morning."

"The priest, too?"

"Yeah. We just sat. She didn't say a word, but I felt I came to understand her well. Sitting, I could hear the master's voice in my belly."

"Really?"

I put the tapes back in the paper bag, and Ryokai continued, "I realized I had not been serious enough. I had forgotten that it was I myself who had decided to become a monk. Somehow I'd gotten the idea that someone else had made me do it."

I nodded.

"I don't listen to music here. If I want to hear music, I recite the sutras in a loud voice. Then, this

morning, my master told me that my beating out the time during sutra recitation had improved. I hadn't expected it, and it sure made me happy."

"That's great, it really is." The priest had noticed all right; she must have been waiting for the right time to tell him.

"Don't worry about me," he turned his intense eyes toward me. "And also please tell mother not to worry."

"Okay."

The story of Priest Tozan flashed through my mind. Perhaps Ryokai had heard it. Maybe in his belly during zazen. I realized I should now be ready to close the door that stands before me. I felt glad, yet lonely. Looking at his shaven head as he went back to his sweeping, now I could clearly see him as Gyokusen Ryokai.

When I returned home my wife was out on the veranda, staring into the distance. I approached her, full of things to say, but then stopped dead in my tracks: even though I drew near, she didn't turn toward me. Not even the strains of "Jesu Joy of Man's Desiring," which she constantly hummed, could be heard.

"I asked her to really train him well," I spoke in a casual tone. "The priest promised me she would make him continue his training no matter what. I believe she'll risk her life for it," I said, as the image of the priest sitting through the night with Ryokai came to mind. Near seventy, and with her body racked with illness, it must have been damned hard.

In silence, my wife placed her arms on the ledge of

the veranda, arched her back and rested her chin on top of her hands. In her younger days, her face had looked really charming under a Western-style red hat, her cool eyes absorbed in the distance. Now, she had a gaunt air about her. I wonder what ever became of that hat. That was long ago, before Ryokai was even born, before I had begun Zen practice. Why had I begun Zen practice, anyway?

I looked off into the distance myself, then collected my thoughts and, putting my hands on the ledge next to her, said, "Now all we can do is trust the priest."

"Nobody's asking you to do that," she suddenly spoke up, still staring off into the distance. "I'm not worried about his training. You always say such things, but it's quite beside the point. I've never doubted the priest. If she says she'll make him a fine monk, I'm sure she will. And that's fine with me. I've already given him up to her, so it's fine with me. Can we trust the priest or not?—that's your problem."

I'd blown it again. I stood there as if my hands were glued to the ledge. Coming up over the hill, the breeze on this summer evening struck my cheeks as it passed by. A feeling of loneliness crept over me. My son, and my wife, too, have gone out of my reach, making me feel like I'm once again wandering around lost in a foreign country. Maybe I've been walking alone all along.

In the breeze I heard the priest's voice: "Just Mu. The seer, the seeing, and the seen are all Mu."

"It doesn't matter," my wife said, as if partly to comfort me, and partly to persuade herself. She added, "It's no use moping around forever. I've got to get on with my life. I've decided to look to the future, as you said. I'll believe anything anyone tells me."

Stretching and leaning over the ledge, she waved her hand. I wondered for a moment if she were waving to the future. Then, looking down, I saw a figure appearing and disappearing from between the row of camphor trees. It was Rie, in a blue T-shirt, white, pleated skirt, and matching socks. That briskly moving figure is the future dancing, for sure. She must have been returning from cram school, carrying her cloth bag full of books. My wife was not standing out here on the veranda lost in memories of our son; she was awaiting our daughter's return. It seems recently she had been devoted to taking care of Rie.

Our daughter looked up at us as she walked. She resembles my wife in her youth. With dark eyebrows and eyes, her facial features stand out even at a distance. By the self-conscious, reluctant way she waves back, I can see she's already grown up. She's almost as big as our son was when he entered the temple.

Standing by my wife and waving to Rie, I found myself thinking that maybe it was about time our daughter began training too.

ABOUT THE AUTHOR

The author, **Kiyohiro Miura,** was born in Hokkaido in 1930. After enrolling in the education department of Tokyo University, he went to the United States, where he earned a degree in creative writing from the University of Iowa. Currently a professor in Meiji University's engineering department, he is also the author of *California Song (Kariforunia no Uta)*, *Into the English Fog (Igirisu no Kiri no Naka e)*, and *Literary Training for the Spirit: America and Me (Bungaku Shugyo—Amerika to Watashi)*.

ABOUT THE TRANSLATOR

Jeff Shore, born and raised in the Philadelphia area, has undertaken Zen study and practice for twenty-five years, the last fifteen in Japan. He is presently Associate Professor of English and Zen Buddhism at Hanazono University in Kyoto. He has written and lectured extensively on Zen, and his English translations have appeared in leading journals on Buddhism and Japanese culture, including *Chanoyu Quarterly* and *The Eastern Buddhist*.